TEAMWORK

Sage's *Series in Interpersonal Communication* is designed to capture the breadth and depth of knowledge emanating from scientific examinations of face-to-face interaction. As such, the volumes in this series address the cognitive and overt behavior manifested by communicators as they pursue various conversational outcomes. The application of research findings to specific types of interpersonal relationships (e.g., marital, managerial) is also an important dimension of this series.

SAGE SERIES IN
INTERPERSONAL COMMUNICATION
Mark L. Knapp, Series Editor

TeamWork

WHAT MUST GO RIGHT / WHAT CAN GO WRONG

CARL E. LARSON
FRANK M. J. LaFASTO

Sage Series

Interpersonal Communication 10

SAGE PUBLICATIONS
The International Professional Publishers
Newbury Park   London   New Delhi

To Alexander, Nicholas,
Jonathan and Spencer—
One Great Team!

For information address:

SAGE Publications, Inc.
2111 West Hillcrest Drive
Newbury Park, California 91320

SAGE Publications Ltd.
28 Banner Street
London EC1Y 8QE
England

SAGE Publications India Pvt. Ltd.
M-32 Market
Greater Kailash I
New Delhi 110 048 India

Printed in the United States of America

Library of Congress Cataloging-in-Publication Data

Larson, Carl E.
    Teamwork : what must go right, what can go wrong / Carl E. Larson
and Frank M.J. LaFasto.
        p.   cm.—(Sage series in interpersonal communication ; v.
10)
    Bibliography: p.
    Includes index.
    ISBN 0-8039-3289-8.—ISBN 0-8039-3290-1 (pbk.)
    1. Work groups.   I. LaFasto, Frank M. J.   II. Title.
III. Series.
HD66.L37   1989
658.4'036—dc20   89-32444
                                                        CIP

FIFTH PRINTING 1990

CONTENTS

SERIES EDITOR'S INTRODUCTION

Studies of cross-cultural values and behavior leave little doubt that the United States manifests an individualistic, rather than collectivistic, orientation (Gudykunst & Ting-Toomey, 1988). It is not surprising, then, to observe that we have traditionally emphasized individual goals and individual leadership. Our bookstores are saturated with volumes focusing on individual initiative and individual achievement. This book is different. Here the focus is on individuals who are asked (or volunteer) to function as a team.

I believe this book has enormous significance. Virtually everyone who reads this book has had experiences with teams—sometimes frustrating, sometimes gratifying, and sometimes puzzling. We may wonder why something as intangible as "team spirit" or a feeling of "teamwork" develops in some teams and not others. But whether we understand the subtleties of team functioning or not, most of us are aware of the critical role teams play in our lives—in getting work accomplished and in solving problems. In this sense, then, there is a practical significance associated with our learning about team effectiveness (and ineffectiveness) in our daily work lives. It is also clear that the problems facing our local communities, commercial organizations, and our national government will increasingly require the input and jointly coordinated action from several people—that is, a team. And, as the complexity of these problems increases, the consequences of ineffective solutions correspondingly increases. Thus, an understanding of teamwork is a fundamental step in assuring our future survival.

With the preceding perspectives in mind, Larson and LaFasto undertook a three-year study of teams with one central question: What are the secrets of successful teams? To answer this question, they interviewed the leaders and members of an extraordinarily diverse range of teams, including the McDonald's Chicken McNugget team, the space shuttle *Challenger* investigation team, the crew of the USS *Kitty Hawk*, executive management teams, cardiac surgery teams, mountain-climbing teams, epidemiology teams from the Centers for Disease Control, and the 1966 Notre Dame championship football team. The book is peppered with fascinating and illuminating quotes from these team members.

What they discovered was a surprising consistency in the characteristics of effective teams. What makes the USS *Kitty Hawk*'s 5,000-person crew work well together as a precision unit is not all that different from what made the 1966 Notre Dame football team national champions. The eight characteristics which explain how and why effective teams develop are:

- A clear, elevating goal
- A results-driven structure
- Competent team members
- Unified commitment
- A collaborative climate
- Standards of excellence
- External support and recognition
- Principled leadership

Having identified the crucial factors associated with team success, the authors developed performance measures to monitor and provide feedback to 32 real-life management teams. The utility of this book for the analysis of ongoing teams is clear, but the book also serves other readers as well. Scholars will find a testable theory of team functioning and a rich corpus of data from which communication researchers can develop hypotheses about the kind of message behavior which might be linked to various team functions.

Who should read this book? Virtually anyone who is in the position of appointing or serving on teams; virtually anyone who is interested in studying the processes and effects of teams; virtually everyone.

—Mark L. Knapp

Gudykunst, W. B., & Ting-Toomey, S. (1988). *Culture and interpersonal communication.* Newbury Park, CA: Sage.

ACKNOWLEDGMENTS

We are grateful to our friends and colleagues for their encouragement and support during the course of this project.

Vern Loucks, chairman and CEO of Baxter International, supported the original "team excellence" project and believed in it enough to give it a whirl with his own senior management committee. Anthony Rucci, who believed in the potential of this project from the beginning, was a constant source of inspiration and leadership. Our many colleagues at Baxter International, particularly those in the Human Resources function, embraced and "role-modeled" the concepts suggested by our research, and they carried the message to others. Mel Ingold provided continual insights as he applied our research to management teams. Our colleagues in the Department of Speech Communication at the University of Denver were a source of ideas and a willing laboratory for testing their implications. Alvin Goldberg and Susan Stein always found the best that could be made of our ideas, and helped us translate them into concrete applications. Tom Cody graciously shared his invaluable experience. Geri Schulz showed limitless flexibility, good humor, and skill as she made unending arrangements, transcribed the interview tapes, and kept our efforts well-organized. Darla Germeroth and Rob Coleman provided the kind of research and tactical support which made this project always interesting and occasionally even fun. Barbara Jensen was a tremendous source of support and unwavering encouragement.

Most of all, we extend our deep appreciation to the team members and leaders we interviewed in the first phase of our research. It is these experts who, by generously sharing their time and insights, made this book possible.

INTRODUCTION

Our original objective was quite different from writing a book. We were going to develop a system for: (1) monitoring the degree to which a team is functioning effectively and, (2) providing feedback which helps that team improve its own effectiveness.

We had developed other monitoring/feedback systems before. We had a long-standing interest in acquiring a better theoretical understanding of how human communication functions in collaborative efforts and a pragmatic interest in improving the success of those collaborative efforts. One of us teaches at a university and the other is vice president of Human Resources Planning and Development for a large, multinational corporation.

Our prior projects had taught us that if you are going to evaluate (ultimately to monitor and provide corrective feedback on) anything, from people to programs, you have to start with a clear identification of the criteria, or standard, against which the thing you are evaluating is to be compared. In order to develop a monitoring/feedback system on teams, we had to have answers to some fundamental questions: What are the properties or features of effectively functioning teams? In order to determine whether a team is functioning effectively, what would you look for? The answers to questions such as these would dictate the content of the monitoring/feedback system.

We developed the system. We've used the system to monitor and provide feedback to many ongoing teams. The last chapter of this book reports what we've learned from this process.

But a funny thing happened on the way to constructing the measures. The process of isolating and defining the criteria for "judging" a team resulted in three genuine learnings: (1) We encountered unusual consistency in the features of effective teams, across a wide variety of teams; (2) The criteria which emerged from our research seemed to us so basic, so face-valid, that we became excited about the possibility of actually understanding the significant factors that describe and explain teams and teamwork; (3) The most significant learning grew slowly but steadily throughout our research: We found

ourselves talking with team members and leaders who knew the answers to the questions we were asking. They knew! They didn't just
know *about* teams. They didn't just understand teams intellectually.
They knew teams and teamwork in ways we hadn't even contem-
plated. They had answers to questions we hadn't even sufficient
knowledge to formulate. And we began to appreciate the potential in
summarizing that knowledge.

This book was written in tribute to the team leaders and members
we interviewed in the early stages of our research. Their knowledge
of teams and teamwork deserves special recognition. It is valuable
knowledge. It is knowledge which can make a difference. We sin-
cerely hope that we have, in this book, done it justice.

—Carl E. Larson
—Frank M.J. LaFasto

1

Toward Understanding Teams and Teamwork

> There are many objects of great
> value to man which cannot be
> attained by unconnected
> individuals, but must be attained
> if at all, by association.
>
> Daniel Webster

For several decades now social scientists have been urging us to confront a sad paradox in our collective evolution (e.g., Zimbardo & Ebbeson, 1969, chap. 1). On the one hand, we possess the technical competence, physical resources, and intellectual capacity to satisfy all the basic needs of mankind. There is little question that we have the wherewithal to provide food, clothing, and shelter for every individual on this planet. In fact, having spent more than three years studying teams and team achievement for this project, we now find it difficult to identify any goal that the collective "we" would be incapable of achieving.

On the other hand, we seem to lack the essential ability to work together effectively to solve critical problems. In fact, the potential for collective problem-solving is so often unrealized and the promise of collective achievement so often unfulfilled, that we exhibit what seems to be a developmental disability in the area of social competence. The potential is there. The realization of that potential too often is not.

Our lack of ability to collaborate successfully has been lamented by Donald Straus, who after serving as a professional arbitrator and president of the American Arbitration Association, was compelled to write that the long-range consequences of our problem-solving efforts will produce only "losers."

As an example of our inability to work together, Straus cited the issue of acid rain, an environmental phenomenon that can pollute lakes, kill fish, and destroy vegetation. Straus observed that, sadly, controversy and an emphasis on individual rather than a collective agenda have impeded progress in solving this potentially tragic—but ultimately solvable—problem. Straus (1986) writes that the parties involved in the disputes:

> Consider the information available to them as weapons for seeking victories rather than as tools for understanding the problems. They will only share information that they believe to be helpful in the pursuit of their current goals, and usually these goals will be narrowly focused and (of) short-term. (p. 156)

Two years after Straus's lament, consensus began to emerge around another, perhaps even more serious problem—the so-called greenhouse effect—a gradual warming of the planet caused by chemical changes in the atmosphere. A bipartisan coalition of senators issued a warning that catastrophe will inevitably follow inaction in responding to the threat of global warming ("Wirth Maps," 1988). Senator Tim Wirth of Colorado stated that the greenhouse effect is the most significant economic, political, environmental, and human problem facing the twenty-first century. And Senator John Chaffee of Rhode Island called global warming the single greatest threat facing the world today.

Because this book was written in the fall of 1988, the eventual outcomes related to these two problems, acid rain and the greenhouse effect, remain uncertain. What becomes increasingly clear is the old paradox: Our ability to collaborate effectively in developing and implementing concrete responses to these problems lags far behind our ability to detect the environmental damage and document the increasing severity of the problems.

Clearly, if we are to solve the enormous problems facing our society, we need to learn how to collaborate more effectively. We need to know how to set aside individual agendas so that a common understanding of a problem has an opportunity to develop. We need to understand how that common understanding gets translated into concrete performance objectives so that a realistic and attainable solution to a problem becomes identified. We need to know how the activities of people can be coordinated and their efforts brought together within a structure that integrates and focuses, rather than diffuses. We need to know how to foster the trust and the sharing of information that will lead to the best decisions—decisions that will have the maximum impact on the problem and lead to the minimum disruption of individual lives.

We do not denigrate the significance of individual thinking and creativity in solving problems. We simply acknowledge that the problems that confront us are so complex that we must go one step further and demand that our thoughtful, creative individuals "put their heads together" to reach the best possible solutions.

THE GROWING COMPLEXITY OF PROBLEMS

On December 17, 1903, on a sandy beach near Kitty Hawk, North Carolina, Orville Wright piloted the Wright Flyer on an historic flight that covered 120 feet. The Wright brothers, Orville and Wilbur, had designed and constructed the Wright Flyer in their bicycle shop, in the space that could be salvaged from the demands of running a business. That short flight will probably always be regarded as one of the marvelous achievements of mankind.

Contrast this to the development of the Boeing 747. The 747 project had an early budget of about $1 billion, and a five-year time line. The following excerpt from our interview with Joe Sutter, director of the 747 project, reminds us that growth is an essential component in the success of any endeavor and that growth inevitably brings complexity.

Sutter: When we started to deliver the airplanes the recession was on, and the airlines were slow to take the airplanes. The company got down to where they really needed the money. They knew they were betting the company on the project's success.

We: What was it about the project itself or the airplane that made it worth that risk?

Sutter: In any kind of endeavor, if you aren't growing, you're dying. The airplane business itself is mature now. Look at the struggle Douglas and Lockheed have had to try to stay in it. What was

important, I think, was just the decision that this is the business
we are in, and we want to stay in it, and we have to grow with it
and be leaders. Just the commitment to stay in the business.
Boeing has always been willing to take the risk of advanced
technology, not for the purpose of advancing technology, but
for the promise of coming up with a better product.

We think Joe Sutter is right. In any endeavor—aviation technology
or government, professional football or epidemiology—growth is, at
the very least, inevitable and necessary for survival. But growth
brings complexity. Almost nothing, living or otherwise, grows in the
direction of simplicity.

Organizational theorist Perrow (1984) has argued that technological systems have become so complex that we should expect failures of
disastrous proportions as a result of failures of system components.
Indeed, the space shuttle *Challenger* disaster, though directly caused
by the failure of the "O-ring" (one of 748 items on the shuttle identified by the investigative team as individually capable of causing the
loss of the shuttle) may well have been contributed to by the complexity of the decision-making structure of the Mission Management
Team.

Growth in complexity becomes magnified when the coordination is
not only within, but between organizations. One outstanding example is Microelectronics and Computer Technology Corporation
(MCC), which has brought together a group of leading companies—
including Boeing, Harris, Honeywell, Lockheed, 3M, RCA, and
Sperry—to meet the challenge of foreign competition in high technology. MCC head Bobby Ray Inman foresees collaborative efforts occurring within other industries as well—including energy, chemicals,
and perhaps even steel—as a way of accelerating research no individual company would be willing to undertake on its own (Keidel, 1985,
p. 166). Regardless of the success or failure of MCC, large-scale
collaborative efforts within high technology are likely to continue.
The high technology market is advancing far too rapidly for any one
company to control it.

Even in endeavors in which autonomy seems great and individual
responsibility for action might be presumed commonplace, complexity and the need for collaboration are becoming irrefutable facts of
life. Consider the following description of health-care delivery, written more than a decade ago (Eichhorn, 1974):

The use of interdisciplinary teams for health care delivery has accelerated due to the increasingly complex and broadening definition of health care. Whereas earlier, health care was confined to the treatment of disease, health care is now defined in terms of total human well-being, and addresses itself to the maintenance of health and the prevention of disease.

This new mission of health systems has called attention to economic, social psychological and environmental aspects of life that impact upon health. With the acceptance of this broad definition, organizational forms for health delivery have begun to change responsively. Because health problems have become defined in complex and multi-faceted terms, health organizations have discovered it is necessary to have the information and skills of many disciplines in order to develop valid solutions and deliver comprehensive care to individuals and families. (p. 13)

Whatever the problems are that occupy our attention, it is probable that the more significant they are to our collective well-being or to the success of our institutions and enterprises, the more complex they are likely to be. Solving these complex problems demands the integration of many divergent points of view and the effective collaboration of many individuals. Bennis and Nanus (1985) concluded from their study of successful leaders that traditional information sources and management techniques have become less effective or even obsolete. "Linear information, linear thinking, and incremental strategies are no match for the turbulence of today's business climate" (p. 10).

THE CONTRIBUTION OF INDIVIDUALS THROUGH COLLABORATION

As both the problems that confront us and the solutions we develop become more complex, the means through which we are able to affect outcomes must also change. Robert Reich (1987) observes in *Tales of a New America:*

Rarely do even Big Ideas emerge any longer from the solitary labors of genius. Modern science and technology is too complicated for one brain. It requires groups of astronomers, physicists, and computer pro-

grammers to discover new dimensions of the universe; teams of micro-
biologists, oncologists, and chemists to unravel the mysteries of cancer.
With ever more frequency. Nobel prizes are awarded to collections of
people. Scientific papers are authored by small platoons of researchers.
(p. 126)

The pattern Reich describes in research activities has been noted in
the industrial arena as well. In fact, recognition of this pattern in
American industry was regarded as newsworthy by *The New York
Times*, which reported a considerable increase in the formation of
teams and the adoption of collaborative strategies in the auto, steel,
and textile industries (Holusha, 1987).

The futurist Toffler (1980) saw an even broader pattern when he
described the organization of the future in *The Third Wave*:

> . . . as we shift to the new principles and begin to apply them together,
> we are necessarily led to wholly new kinds of organizations for the
> future. These Third Wave organizations have flatter hierarchies. They
> are less top-heavy. They consist of small components linked together in
> temporary configurations. Each of these components has its own rela-
> tionship with the outside world, its own foreign policy, so to speak,
> which it maintains without having to go through the center. These
> organizations operate more and more around the clock. (p. 263)

This emerging pattern of organization is described by Reich as a
new "tale" of America, by *The New York Times* as a new "spirit" in
industry, and by Toffler as the "organization of the future." In the
"new organization," individual contributions will come as a result of
understanding how one's efforts coincide with others, how one's objectives can be integrated with those of others, how one's own point
of view can be advanced at the same time that other points of view are
understood and acknowledged, and how multiple motives and energies can be focused on a single performance objective. In short, our
contributions increasingly will come as a result of our ability to understand teams and teamwork.

A STRATEGY FOR UNDERSTANDING TEAMS AND TEAMWORK

Our point of departure for understanding teams and teamwork was
to ask a question: What are the characteristics, features, or attributes

of effectively functioning teams? We assumed that the corollary question—What explains or accounts for teams that function ineffectively?—could be answered at the same time that we pursued the answer to the first question.

Our first step was to identify and synthesize the prior research on team effectiveness. Most of that research came from social science and organizational development sources. Most was very narrowly focused, usually on psychological factors, such as feelings of cohesiveness among members of sports teams. We will refer to this research at appropriate points, such as during our discussion of the emotional "climate" that may exist within a team, but the prior research was clearly insufficient to understand fully the features or characteristics of effectively functioning teams.

We adopted a very broad definition of team: A team has two or more people; it has a specific performance objective or recognizable goal to be attained; and coordination of activity among the members of the team is required for the attainment of the team goal or objective. This definition eliminates from theoretical interest many groups that are commonly called "teams." For example, there are many well-known sports teams, such as Davis Cup tennis, in which individual matches are played against members of another team, and points or wins/losses are awarded on the basis of the number of individual matches in which a team is victorious. But because there is, in many of these teams, no coordination required among the individual members of the team in order for the team to reach its objective or goal, these teams fall outside the boundaries of this research.

Our plan for developing an understanding of teams and teamwork included two phases: (1) We identified a sample of teams noteworthy either for their achievement or for the insight each team would provide into the nature of teamwork. We conducted interviews with the leaders and/or members of these teams. From these interviews we identified the distinguishing features of effective team performance. (2) We took the distinguishing characteristics of high performance teams, operationalized these characteristics into a set of measures, and used these measures to monitor and provide feedback to 32 management teams.

This plan took about three years to fulfill. Although it involved a variety of methods and procedures, we were guided more by the method of inquiry known as "grounded theory" than by any other systematic research strategy (Glaser & Strauss. 1967). Perhaps our general strategy will be best understood if we simply describe what we did.

A "THEORETICALLY RICH" SAMPLE OF TEAMS

A traditional sampling plan, one that emphasizes representativeness, would have as its objective the description of a broad *population* of teams on the basis of a smaller but representative *sample* of those teams. This was not our purpose. Even had it been possible to do so, we would not have attempted a random sampling of teams for the purpose of describing what the typical team is like.

This type of random sampling is valuable for describing populations, such as voter preferences. However, there are some phenomena, such as creativity, about which a random sample of the general population will tell you very little. The way to investigate creativity is to study case after case of creative people to determine the properties of creativity.

We pursued, therefore, a sampling strategy that grounded theorists refer to as "theoretical sampling." Our strategy was to handpick teams—in a sense because of their nonrepresentativeness—which would provide us with the greatest theoretical insight into what characterizes effectively functioning teams. Furthermore, this handpicking of the sample was continuous. Later sampling decisions were guided in part by what we had discovered about the nature of effectively functioning teams from earlier sampling decisions. That is, having obtained some insight into space teams, we wanted to see whether these insights changed greatly, in minor ways, or not at all when we moved to cardiac surgery teams, then to championship college football teams, then to epidemiology teams, and so forth.

A theoretical sampling plan unfolded as the research progressed. Our basic strategy was to vary the cases examined and to keep track of the properties being discovered as the sample unfolded. Although grounded theory does not offer a clearly defined "plan" for theoretical sampling, the plan we created went through three stages: divergence, testing, and saturation.

1. Divergence. Our first objective was to identify a relatively widespread, divergent sample of teams and then to see whether the properties of these effectively functioning teams appeared with any consistency. Our point of departure for phase one was an interview with Joe Jaworski, founder and chairman of the American Leadership Forum.

We not only interviewed Jaworski concerning the American Leadership Forum chapters, which we categorized as highly collaborative community action teams, but we also enlisted Jaworski's assistance in helping to identify other teams that might provide us with additional insights into the nature of successful teams. This first phase of the sampling plan developed as follows:

Team	*Interviewee*
American Leadership Forum	Joe Jaworski, founder and chairman
Mt. Everest Expedition/British Antarctic Expedition	George McCleod, member
Mt. Kongur (China) Expedition	Pat Dillingham, member
Presidential Commission on the Space Shuttle Challenger Accident	LTC (USA) Thomas Reinhardt, executive secretary Captain William Bauman, staff writer
U.S. Space Command	Colonel Sam Beamer, one of the original founders and planners
Cardiac Surgery	Dr. Don C. Wukasch, member of Drs. Michael E. DeBakey and Denton A. Cooley surgical teams
Notre Dame Championship Football Team, 1966	Jim Lynch, captain Jim Seymour, member Tom Quinn, member
U.S. Naval Academy Football Team, 1961–1963	Admiral Tom Lynch, captain
Centers for Disease Control Epidemiology Teams	Dr. Michael Gregg, acting director of the Epidemiology Program Office J. Lyle Conrad, MD, director of Field Services, EPO, CDC Atlanta

Two comments about this first phase of sampling: (1) Although these were the teams targeted in the sampling plan, information about a great many other teams emerged from our interviews. For example, Jim Lynch was captain of the 1966 NCAA championship football team for Notre Dame. But Lynch was also the defensive captain of the Kansas City Chiefs, Super Bowl IV Champions; had an NFL defensive unit named after him (the "Lynch Mob"); and is now both a member of one and a leader of another very successful corporate executive management team. So there were a great many more teams discussed in the interviews than the target sample we originally identified. (2) The distinguishing features of effectively functioning teams emerged quickly and with amazing consistency. And while the properties were easily identifiable and almost always present, the specific forms taken by these properties varied from team to team. We found, for example, that effectively functioning teams have a very clear structure and are designed around a desired result or a specific performance objective. The structure is dictated by the result to be attained and is both highly strategic and readily apparent. And though this is a consistent property of effectively functioning teams, the structure differs dramatically between the highly collaborative, trust-based community action teams that make up the American Leadership Forum and the highly technically competent, clear lines of responsibility teams that make up cardiac surgery. In either case, the structure is very well planned and determined exclusively by the results to be attained.

This rapidly emerging consistency in the properties of effectively functioning teams led us quickly to phase two of the theoretical sampling plan.

2. Testing. In the second phase of the sampling plan we moved from divergence to homogeneity. We wanted to see whether the characteristics that emerged in the first phase would adequately describe a narrower, but deeper sample of similar teams. We chose two types of teams for the second phase—executive management teams and project teams.

Executive Management Teams

Team	Interviewee
Baxter International	Vernon R. Loucks, chairman and CEO
The Dun and Bradstreet Corporation	Harrington (Duke) Drake, former chairman and CEO
Emerson Electric Co.	Charles F. Knight, chairman and CEO
Petro-Lewis Corporation	Lon McCain, former CFO
Mt. Sinai Hospital	Ruth Rothstein, CEO
Alvarado Construction	Linda Alvarado, CEO

Project Teams

Team	Interviewee
McDonald's Chicken McNugget Team	E. J. (Bud) Sweeney, team leader
Boeing 747 Airplane Project	Joe Sutter, team leader
Small ICBM (Midgetman) Programs at Boeing	Joe Madden, team leader
Baxter International Merger Team	Anthony J. Rucci, team leader
Honeywell Signal Processing and "Gate Array" Teams	Jerry Anderson, director of sales, DPC Honeywell
IBM PC Team (the "Boca Raton" Team)	Larry Rojas, director of planning

3. Saturation. The second sampling phase convinced us that, especially with respect to executive management and project teams, the properties of successful teams were identifiable and highly consistent. However, in the process of fine-tuning our understanding of the properties and the specific forms those properties might take, we wanted to avoid missing any characteristics that might be important to an understanding of team success. So we moved into a third phase of sampling, called "saturation," in which the objective is to exhaust the theoretical dimensions of the phenomenon being studied. To make sure that we hadn't missed any important properties of successful teams, we spread the sample out again, this time sampling more unusual cases of effectively functioning teams.

Team	Interviewee
Disaster Teams	Tom Drabek, sociologist, disaster researcher
Theater Productions	Paul Lazarus, New York director
USS *Kitty Hawk*	Admiral Ned Hogan, former commander
U.S. Navy Strike Warfare Center	Captain Joe Prueher, developer and First Commander
GAO and Congressional Investigative Teams	Charles Bowsher, Comptroller General of the United States
Presidential Cabinets	The Honorable Elliot Richardson, former Cabinet member

THE INTERVIEWS AND ANALYSES

A set of core questions was asked in every interview. These core questions involved critical incident questions, designed to get the interviewee to recall and describe specific features or characteristics of teams the interviewee had experienced. The core questions asked the individual to recall a specific point in time when he or she was a member of an unusually effectively functioning team; to describe the situation; and to identify those factors, in the opinion of the interviewee, that accounted for this high level of effectiveness. Similarly, another set of core questions asked the individual to recall a specific point in time when he or she was a member of an unusually poorly functioning team; to describe the situation; and to identify the factors that accounted for this low level of effectiveness.

After the initial period of orientation and explanation and after the core questions had been asked, we pursued whatever avenues or insights emerged during the critical incident questions. We were always happy that we had taken a more open-ended stance in the latter part of the interviews. In every case, we were talking to an individual whose knowledge would have been trivialized by a heavily structured interview.

Let us give you one example of what we mean by this. Very early on, in the orientation phase of the interview with Elliot Richardson, we were explaining the purpose of the project. Richardson has been a member of five Presidential Cabinets and is still regarded as one of the most effective Cabinet members and government administrators in recent history. The following is Elliot Richardson's response to our opening statement regarding our interest in finding out what makes teams effective:

> I would say first, the effectiveness of a team is a function, however communicated, of clarity about its purpose.
> Second, the organization should in one way or another convey an appreciation of the people who comprise it. That means not only recognition of their roles, but appreciation of their service, where it is good. It should also entail an intelligent approach to the failures and shortcomings or the deficiencies of its members. In a sense, it is a constructive approach to helping them overcome these. Both aspects imply another ingredient that I have always thought important—namely, the ability to cast people in the role in which they are the most effective.

Third, in addition to clarifying goals and appreciating people, it is important to convey a sense of significance or value of what you are doing and the integrity of your operation. Integrity is not just a morally desirable attribute. A number of years ago I read with considerable care Studs Terkel's interviews on working, and it was striking that the least happy workers were the workers in the sleaziest organizations. They were being asked to do something they didn't feel good about.

Fourth, is a sense that even if the organization is tough, it is managed with a sense of fairness. In other words, the manner in which the rewards and penalties are distributed should be perceived as fair and consistent. Fairness, of course, is related to the appreciation of people.

The last point that occurs to me is communication. Internal communication among the participants keeps current their sense of what the goals are; what progress toward them has been made; and the relationships that they have with the other players and the other parts of the organization.

As Richardson's response illustrates, it was not unusual for an interviewee to anticipate our interests and respond to them, often on target. These were, after all, highly competent and knowledgeable leaders and members of teams, so the interviews tended to be very informative. In addition, in some cases the information from the interviews was supplemented by written materials and even by observation.

Our analysis of this information, more than any other systematic method, followed the constant comparative analysis of grounded theory. We were both present for all interviews. Following each interview we would separately, and then together, identify the properties that the particular interviewee saw as characterizing effective teams. We would then identify the properties that the interviewee saw as differentiating effective from less effective teams. We would identify the specific forms those properties or characteristics assumed, whenever it was possible to do so. We then would compare the properties with those that had emerged from previous interviews. Where the properties differed or the specific forms varied, we would discuss potential reasons for these variations in terms of the nature of the team we had just examined, then extend our sampling plan by another two or three cases, and proceed.[1]

This strategy led us to the identification of eight characteristics, or properties, of effectively functioning teams. The next eight chapters of this book are devoted to those eight properties and their elaboration. In brief, those characteristics are: (1) a clear, elevating goal; (2) a results-driven structure; (3) competent members; (4) unified commitment; (5) a collaborative climate; (6) standards of excellence; (7) external support and recognition; (8) principled leadership.

ANALYSES OF MANAGEMENT TEAMS

The last chapter of this book describes the second phase of the study, a phase that is continuing. Having identified eight characteristics of effectively functioning teams, we took the specifics of those eight characteristics and constructed from them a series of items that formed measures of team effectiveness, leader effectiveness, and the effectiveness of individual contributions. On these measures, leaders and members described their intact teams. This information was then processed and used as the basis for feedback reports. With this feedback system, intact teams analyzed their present status with respect to the eight characteristics of effective team and sought ways to improve their performance. This monitoring and feedback process has been completed on 32 management teams. A summary of the results of these analyses comprises the content of this book's final chapter.

NOTE

1. Deviations from this pattern occurred on several occasions. For example, while in New York or Washington, D.C., it was convenient and possible to conduct an additional interview, but one which more appropriately belonged in a later sampling phase. We conducted such interviews and then analyzed the transcripts later.

2

A Clear, Elevating Goal

It is rare to discover anything in the realm of human behavior that occurs with great consistency. Our sample was relatively small (31 interviews covering more than 75 teams), but very diverse. Therefore, it was surprising to find that in every case, without exception, when an effectively functioning team was identified, it was described by the respondent as having a clear understanding of its objective.

Two insights about teams emerged early, consistently, and very emphatically from our interviews. First, high performance teams have both a clear understanding of the goal to be achieved and a belief that the goal embodies a worthwhile or important result.

Second, whenever an *ineffectively* functioning team was identified and described, the explanation for the team's ineffectiveness involved, in one sense or another, the goal. The goal had become unfocused; the goal had become politicized; the team had lost a sense of urgency or significance about its objective; the team's efforts had become diluted by too many other competing goals; individual goals had taken priority over team goals; and so on. Let's develop the earlier and more consistent conclusion first.

The principle of goal clarity emerged forcefully from our data as it has from other, similar investigations in the past. Garfield's analyses (1986) of peak performers in both athletics and in business led him to identify "the one characteristic that appears in every peak performer I have studied: A sense of mission" (p. 77; see also Garfield & Bennett, 1984). Garfield defined mission as an image of a desired state of affairs that inspires action.

Bennis and Nanus (1985) were equally absolute in their conclusion about the effective leaders that they studied.

All ninety people interviewed had an *agenda*, an unparalleled concern with outcome. Leaders are the most results-oriented individuals in the world, and results get attention. Their visions or intentions are compelling and pull people toward them. Intensity coupled with commitment is magnetic. And these intense personalities do not have to coerce people to pay attention; they are so intent on what they are doing that, like a child completely absorbed with creating a sand castle in a sand box, they draw others in. (p. 28)

Similarly, Truell identified a heavy emphasis on clear objectives in the planning process as an essential feature of effective work teams. In fact, from Dewey in 1910 to Hirokawa and Poole in 1986 the point has been made repeatedly: The more an individual or a group of people have a clear understanding of the nature of a problem that confronts them, the more effective they will be in solving that problem.

GOAL CLARITY

The first and most important characteristic of a goal is clarity. *Clarity* implies that there is a specific performance objective, phrased in such concrete language that it is possible to tell, unequivocally, whether or not that performance objective has been attained. Kiefer and Senge (1984) illustrate goal clarity in the following example:

The Apollo Moon Project provided a superb demonstration of the power of a clear and compelling vision. By committing themselves to "placing a man on the moon by the end of the 1960's," the leaders of the project took a stand. The clarity and conviction they generated touched people at all levels of the enterprise. One can imagine how much less spectacular the results might have been if they had adopted an alternative mission statement, such as "to be leaders in space exploration." Unfortunately, such "motherhood" mission statements are the norm for most organizations. (p. 112)

Examples of goal clarity are literally everywhere in our interviews with leaders and members of effective teams. Tom Quinn, of the 1966 Notre Dame national collegiate football championship team, stated:

The mission was totally clear. There was only one reason to be there that year. That was to win the national championship, period. We believed we could do it; we had great talent, great coaching, and great leadership.

The same kind of clarity was present in the *Challenger* disaster investigation effort. Captain William Bauman, a staff writer for the investigation team, identified goal clarity as one of the primary explanations for the success of the team, one of the most effective Presidential Commissions in recent history.

The mission of the Rogers Commission was to investigate the *Challenger* disaster and determine cause within 120 days—a goal that was frequently reinforced by Chairman Rogers and Executive Director Alton G. Keel, Jr. The team was under considerable pressure from the public and some media to assess blame. Endless accusations, explanations, and cases supporting claims of guilt and innocence might easily have occupied the attention of the Rogers Commission. In fact, these issues are still being explored in legal arenas today.

But what was needed immediately following the disaster was a clear determination of cause. What caused the disaster? What were the major contributing factors? And what specific recommendations would grow from these determinations? The report of the Rogers Commission never deviates from the question of what happened and why. The mission was clear and concrete, and the team was able to execute it effectively.

Paul Lazarus, a producer and director in the theater and in television, has heard many actors talk about good and bad directors. The common criticism of a bad director is that he or she has great difficulty making decisions, is unclear or "wishy-washy" in approach, or is so ambiguous in conception that actors feel they are unable to do their best work.

Lazarus learned an important lesson about goal clarity early in his career:

I learned a terribly good lesson at a relatively young age: It is better to have a clear idea and have it fail than to be unclear in conception, because you can learn from a failure and go on to the next clear idea. But if you never make a commitment to anything with clarity, or care

about it, then you don't get any feedback and you can never know if
the idea was good or bad.

Anthony Rucci, one of the leaders of the team that implemented
the largest merger in the history of the health-care industry (Baxter
Travenol/American Hospital Supply), has a similar focus on clarity in
explaining the success of merger transitions. According to Rucci, the
first, and most important step is to define the objective clearly. In
fact, Rucci believes it is important to be able to visualize the result
and describe what that result will look like once it is accomplished.
For Rucci, the vision includes imagining what excellence would look
like in achieving the result. "It's getting the results in a way that
hasn't been done before. It's achieving the results in a way that sets a
standard, a higher standard for how you can get something done."
   Though we are describing a characteristic—indeed the most consistent characteristic—of effective teams, we were struck by the fact that
this clarity of purpose seemed also to be a characteristic of the people
we interviewed. There was almost no ambiguity or uncertainty on the
part of any of the interviewees related to what they were doing or why.
   Captain Joe Prueher, commander of the Strike Warfare Center
(the Navy center in Fallon, Nevada, that trains airwings in coordinated strike tactics), knows exactly what our national policy is in the
Middle East; what the specific role of the Navy is in implementing
that policy; how the carrier battle group brings the Navy's role to bear
on our national policy; what the specific function of the aircraft carrier is within the aircraft battle group; in what precise terms the
airwing of about 85 airplanes functions as an instrument of our policy;
and how those intact airwings have to be trained to go beyond individual flying and fighting skills to develop effective coordinated tactics.
   Captain Prueher talks about coordinated strike tactics in much the
same way that Paul Lazarus talks about directing stage productions—
with clarity and precision. That's fortunate because the one thing that
an airwing and a theater cast have in common is the need for a clear
understanding of their objective.

A GOAL THAT IS ELEVATING

Recently, we helped a board of directors reorganize itself along the dimensions identified in our research. The team involved was the board of a community agency that serves the developmentally disadvantaged. The individuals served by this agency worked in special businesses that were managed broadly by the agency.

During the discussion of agency goals, one of the board members offered a new goal for the agency: The businesses managed by the agency would become so profitable that they would lose their not-for-profit status under the law. The businesses operating under the agency charter would then have ownership transferred to the developmentally disabled clients served by the agency's programs, and those clients would end up owning the businesses in which they worked.

As the board members began to understand the vision, the effect was like a physical rush. This team saw the opportunity to commit themselves to a goal even more worthwhile than the program-delivery goals they were presently serving. And toward the end of the day-long session, we actually saw the team reconstitute itself; that is, some individuals voluntarily left the team so that other prospective members, who could contribute more effectively to achieving the new goal, could be added.

Such events are rare, but they do happen. We've seen them happen in situations in which a team becomes clear about what it is doing and then struggles with the question of whether it makes a difference if the team reaches its performance objective. In fact, there is research that identifies a relationship between aspiration levels and performance levels, which might lead to the practical advice that one should find team players with lofty and sincere aspirations (e.g., Chlewinski, 1981). If a goal is clearly understood and viewed by team members as important or worthwhile, then many of the other problems reviewed later in this book can be overcome.

In what sense can a goal be elevating? *First*, the goal can be personally challenging—to the individuals and/or to the collective effort. That sense of personal challenge can be discerned in many teams, but is perhaps clearest in mountain-climbing teams. Pat Dillingham said:

It is something that is difficult to put into words. If I attempt to articulate it it would be like something that challenges me so much, and makes me so glad I survived the situations I put myself in, that it

recharges my battery. It makes me feel like I'm surely not going to die
as a person, either physically or mentally. There is no one thing I do
that pushes me to my limits like mountaineering.

That sense of personal challenge must surely have been experienced by Linda Alvarado as well. Alvarado became unhappy with her
experience as a project accountant in a construction company, took
special classes and training to develop highly focused, construction-
related competencies, selected a team very carefully, and within
seven years became CEO of her own construction company, one of
the most successful in the Southwestern United States.

A goal can be elevating because it challenges—stretching the limits
of physical and mental abilities. It offers an opportunity to excel. In
football or cardiac surgery, a goal can provide individuals and teams
with an opportunity to prove what they're capable of doing.

Second, a goal can be elevating in the sense that the performance
objective itself makes a difference—creating a sense of urgency. For
example, epidemiology teams fight about 600 to 1,000 epidemics a
year in the United States, from salmonella to cholera. So effective are
these teams that most of us are not even aware of the occurrence of
epidemics in this country until a very unusual and threatening epidemic, such as AIDS, reminds us of the very real consequences of
effective team functioning.

Similarly, Charles Bowsher, Comptroller General of the United
States, and director of the General Accounting Office, identified a
factor in the investigative teams that inform Congress on important
issues, a factor that Bowsher called "a sense of urgency."

In 1984, when Central America was heating up we did a job in Honduras to determine whether some new American airfields and installa-
tions were permanent or temporary, because members of Congress
were wondering what the U.S. government was doing down there. The
Pentagon said, "Oh, we're just putting in a temporary airfield and
building, and don't worry about it." Our people went to Honduras, did
an investigation, and immediately came back to brief members of Congress and their staffs and tell them the facilities appeared permanent.
There was no doubt that at that time Congress needed to know right
then what was happening. Congress wanted to act and it matters
whether congressional decisions are based on valid information. That
gave our work an immediacy that made it exciting.

Providing sound information matters most of all to the teams that are charged with discovering what that valid information is—on the basis of which decisions can be made or actions taken. Bowsher continued:

> You can go to the Norfolk Naval Base or Fort Bragg anytime to do an inventory and find all kinds of problems. I've got people that spend a lot of time doing that kind of work. A couple of years ago Senator Wilson got interested in some significant losses from these inventories and the question was where was that stuff going? We investigated and found out some of it was going to Iran. Some of it was going to right-wing organizations and terrorist groups. Suddenly our inventory work become much more exciting to the people who were working on it—there was a greater sense of urgency. And you feel the difference that kind of a sense of urgency makes.

When people are doing something that clearly makes a difference to them, this sense of urgency is present. It shows up in many different ways. Teams lose their sense of time. They discover to their surprise that it's dark outside and they worked right through the supper hours. The rate of communication among team members increases dramatically, even to the point that individuals call each other at all hours of the night because they can't get something out of their minds. There is a sense of great excitement and feelings of elation whenever even minor progress is made toward the goal. There is a lessening of status or positional differences and increased value placed on how much an individual is contributing to the team's success. The focus is squarely on the result the team is pursuing and the progress that is being made, because whether or not the team succeeds clearly makes a difference.

THE MOST FREQUENT EXPLANATION FOR TEAM FAILURE

A clear, elevating goal was always present in the examples of effectively functioning teams described by the respondents. And with almost as much consistency, in the descriptions of ineffectively functioning teams the factor that occurred far more frequently than any other was very simple: The team had raised—or had allowed to become raised—some other issue or focus above the team's performance objective. Something was being attended to that had assumed, at least at that time, a higher priority than the team's goal.

It may have been a control issue, as when people concern themselves more with questions of who's in charge than with finding the best solution to a problem. It may have been a political issue, as when individuals worry more about how others might respond to or feel about the action taken than about whether the action is effective in achieving a goal. It may have been an individual agenda issue, as when members of a team are more concerned with protecting themselves or obtaining personal advantages than with the success of the collective endeavor. Whatever this other factor or issue was, it occupied the team's attention, and the performance objective became de-emphasized. This shifting of priorities occurs so frequently and is such a powerful predictor of decreased team effectiveness that in our work with intact teams, whenever we encounter a team that is functioning poorly we always ask first: What is it that this team is elevating above its performance objective?

Consider the following example of this phenomenon that comes from Jim Seymour's experience. We asked Seymour, a member of the 1966 Notre Dame national championship collegiate football team, if he could recall a time when any of the teams he had been on functioned unusually poorly. He responded with the following case:

When I first joined the Bears, I saw an interesting transition. In '69 the Bears were one and 13. I was traded from the Los Angeles Rams to the Bears in '70. We finished the season six and eight, and we had won the last couple of games. So going into the '71 season we were pretty confident. At the midway point in the '71 season—that's when we played 14 league games—we were five and two, tied for first place with the Minnesota Vikings. The guys were getting nicked here and there but working hard. Everyone had one thing in mind, one goal: Let's win this division, and if we can get to the playoffs, we won't lose in the playoffs. The incentive at that point was money. If you could get into the playoffs and win and go to the Super Bowl, you could make more than most guys make all year.

The coaches got into infighting. They knew that the head coach was not on good grounds with the owner. They started jockeying for position. They forgot what their real goal was, of getting through the season and into the playoffs. They lost the next game. Instead of saying, we lost this one, let's forget about it, review our mistakes on Tuesday and get back on track again, they got worried and started pressing, and we lost the next week. We lost seven games in a row and went to last place. The coaches got desperate. The infighting started some more; it totally tore the team apart.

I will never forget, after the last game the guys didn't even want to stick around. One guy had a U-Haul packed with all his goods, and he was getting out of town. Some of the guys wouldn't even shower after the game. They had cabs waiting to get them to the airport. After the '71 season it was get out of town.

What got elevated above the goal? Personal success. And though the factor that gets elevated may vary, the pattern is consistent case after case. Paul Lazarus recalled an experience he had in one of his first opportunities to direct a stage production. There was an older, veteran actor in the cast who had a conception of the play that was markedly different from that held by Lazarus. It was early in his career, and Lazarus did something he said he would never allow to happen again. He allowed the two conceptions of the play, or goals, to be pursued simultaneously, the actor pursuing one conception and the director pursuing another. Allowing the two conceptions to compete confused the performance of the play. The solution? Replace the actor.

Given the kind of problem and system complexity described in Chapter 1, we noted with increasing interest throughout the interviews how easily teams and/or their leaders can become distracted from their goals. There are so many things to attend to and pressures to respond to that it's not as easy to concentrate on the goal as one might expect—even if the goal is clear and elevating.

One of the more interesting insights we obtained into this phenomenon came when former Cabinet member Elliot Richardson was asked to recall a time when he was a member of an ineffectively functioning team. His example follows:

In the case of the White House, after the onset of the troubles surrounding Watergate, we had in the first place a leader who had lost concentration. The primary purposes of the team were drawn off into the effort to cope, one way or another, with this sea of problems that was rising day by day. That, in turn, was associated with an "us versus them" mentality that you can't have in public service. or indeed any organization. and have it work most effectively.

I was Attorney General during part of that period. and I had been responsible for the recruitment of Archie Cox [as independent prosecutor in the Watergate investigation]. I was constantly dealing with people in the White House who were convinced. starting with the President. that Cox was trying to "get" Nixon. They just wouldn't believe that Cox would rather cut off his right arm than distort or fabricate a case just to "get" anybody. It would have been far better to take for granted that Cox had a job to do and that he would do what the President told him initially he wanted done. namely to have the situation investigated. and to have every lead followed to its end. even if it led to the White House. If the President had been clearer in his own focus on the situation. he could have done any number of things more effectively.

We discovered. both in our interviews and in our later work with intact teams. that this historical example is hardly unique. Leaders and teams lose their focus or concentration quite frequently. Academic deans. for example. lose sight of the fact that they are part of an administrative structure that supports the pursuit of educational goals by faculty and students. The quality of that educational experience too frequently gets de-emphasized, as higher priority is given to territoriality. size of budget. favorable standing with higher administrators. and a dozen other factors that are both more seductive and easier to resolve than the problems associated with improving the quality of the educational experience for the student.

Academia. business. sports. the military—there is no context in which this confusion of priorities does not occur. Moreover. the problem of unfocused goals shows up in endless forms and variety. Admiral Ned Hogan was chief test pilot of the Navy in 1982 to 1985 and was commanding officer of the USS *Kitty Hawk* in 1976 to 1978. When we asked him if he could recall a time when he was a member of an ineffectively functioning team. his answer was "No" and his discussion of his experiences primarily concerned projects involving the development of military airplanes.

Admiral Hogan did describe problems of technology transfer, problems in the military acquisition process. problems in meeting schedules—all bureaucratic issues that impacted the goal of developing the airplane around performance criteria:

At some point in time the customer that you are trying to satisfy gets lost—the kid that's sitting in the cockpit of the airplane. That's who you are trying to satisfy. His environment is very focused. His satisfaction is related to how the vehicle performs, throttle and stick, and what kind of displays you give him to help him do the job he has got to do. He's interested in the aircraft and system performance.

This loss of focus on the goal does not necessarily occur as the result of incompetence, lack of ethics or morality, character flaws, or any other simple explanation. Rather, it occurs because the problems are complex, the strategies for solving the problems are even more complex, and the degree of collaboration required by the problem-solving strategies involves intense and constant concentration in order for the goal to be attained.

We followed with interest the Federal Aviation Administration's investigations of safety-related incidents in the operation of Delta Airlines during the summer of 1987. A report of the agency safety team's conclusions related the following interesting analysis: "There is no evidence that Delta's crews are (on the whole) either unprofessional or purposefully negligent. Rather, it was observed that crew members are frequently acting as individuals rather than as members of a smoothly functioning team" (Witkin, 1987, p. 1).

POLITICS AND PERSONAL AGENDA

The loss of focus or concentration on the goal by team members and leaders can come from a variety of factors. However, our interviews suggest that the predominant factors are politics and individuals agenda.

- Charles F. Knight, chairman and CEO of Emerson Electric, says that managers become ineffective when they start worrying about promotions and how many people they have reporting to them.
- When Harrington (Duke) Drake took over Dun and Bradstreet in 1975, his first priority was to build an effective team. He observed that, "A breath of fresh air went through the organization when we got rid of the politicians."
- Vernon Loucks, chairman and CEO of Baxter International, identified politics as one of the most serious threats to team effectiveness. "When

politics takes over for substance, there is a different channeling of the energies. As soon as politics get into it, you start mistrusting what people are doing. Then the whole thing starts unraveling."

- Tom Drabek, a specialist in disasters, observed that one of the primary differences between effective and ineffective disaster teams is something simple but very important. The effective teams, among other things, have a problem-oriented approach to decision-making. They stay focused on the problem and, as a team, examine the various options in order to respond most effectively. The ineffective teams frequently become embroiled in questions of who's in charge and use the crisis to rationalize an autocratic decision-making style.

- George McLeod indicated that the least effective mountaineering and exploration teams he has been on were those in which a lot of "skiving" occurred. Skiving is McLeod's term for behavior that is designed to conserve strength and/or resources so that individuals can accomplish personal rather than team objectives.

- Anthony Rucci noted that in corporate teams, when things become particularly difficult or threatening—as during a merger—the uncertainty and ambiguity can cause a much more exaggerated, egocentric view of the world. Some people, in an attempt to secure their own position, become dysfunctional. Oddly enough, other people "seem to have an ability to step outside their own personal fears and concerns and stay professional, and more importantly, 'other-oriented.' These people have internal standards about what excellence looks like and what their role ought to be."

Politics and personal agenda seem to be the greatest threats to goal clarity and, consequently, to effective teamwork. But whatever form the threat to goal clarity takes, it must be recognized and combated. As Duke Drake said, "The minute the politicians take over and start worrying about what's in it for me, you're dead in the water."

3

Results-Driven Structure

A key factor differentiating high- and low-success teams is the structure of the team itself. Furthermore, our interviews revealed that when there is a structural or design deficiency, it is typically identified at the most inopportune time. Consider the following example related by Dr. Thomas Drabek, a leading expert on disasters. Dr. Drabek tells of a tragedy that might have been averted during a flash flood in Texas if the rescuers had been able to coordinate better their lifesaving efforts.

> I can recall the frustration in the sheriff's voice as he told of standing at the edge of a very dangerous river where flooding was occurring. He said he would never forget his sense of helplessness at seeing a woman in a tree being battered by the water while hanging onto a limb. Above were two helicopters—one from a state agency, the other from a military agency—and he (the sheriff) was standing there with his radio in his cruiser, but he was on a frequency that could only connect with his office.
>
> He called his office on his radio and tried to tell them where this woman was. The helicopters were going up and down the river and actually rescuing people out of trees. This woman, however, was underneath a bunch of limbs, and could not be seen from above. The helicopters were above him, and the woman was in front of him in the middle of the river, but there was no way he could talk to the pilot. The helicopter finally went by. The woman let go and was drowned. The next day, the sheriff went out and bought CB radios for himself and the pilots.

Effective team structure might be as basic and as simple as the communication required for the coordination of activities. During a disaster, or for that matter any crisis, the absence of such fundamental ingredients as communication channels, or division of labor, or clear authority becomes readily and painfully apparent. However, effective structure is more than merely having the basic components in place. There are times when an abundance of structure can be just as problematic as too little structure.

In January 1986, the space shuttle *Challenger* exploded during take-off, claiming the lives of all seven passengers. The Rogers Commission, the highly acclaimed space shuttle disaster investigation team, identified the cause of the accident as the failure of a rubber "O-ring." One member of the investigation team was Joe Sutter (leader of the Boeing 747 project team). He offered the following observations regarding the "level system"—the review structure for the Mission Management Team:

> That level system is dynamite. It was one thing wrong with NASA. Three days into the hearings they said they knew they had trouble with "the joints," and they decided that it was good enough to fly because it was a "level-three" matter. I said, "A safety matter is a level-three matter?" In effect, the level system stopped the safety discussion right at level three. It was never taken up. That level system is one of the big things wrong with NASA. It is so complex that it restricts communication on important matters.

The importance of structure is not in its presence or absence, nor in having structure for structure's sake. Rather, the significance of structure lies in identifying the appropriate structure for the achievement of a specific performance objective—a configuration that does not confuse effort with results and that makes sense to the team members involved. One of the earliest discoveries in our research was that the same performance objective can be supported by different structural designs, as long as the design moves the team toward the performance objective.

Think about a group of people trying to climb a mountain. In the broadest sense, the goal is to try to reach the top of the mountain. According to the criteria established in Chapter 2, this objective would be fairly clear and straightforward and would seem to be elevating in terms of an opportunity to achieve a sense of personal accomplishment by stretching one's individual limits. The clarity and inspiring nature of the goal is fairly easy to put our finger on.

Such ease quickly vanishes, however, when we begin thinking about how to structure the team to accomplish this objective. Should all members make it to the top of the mountain? Or, is it sufficient for one member of the group to establish the team's flag on the peak? What's more, is it important to reach the top of the mountain at all? Or, could achievement be measured by getting the entire team as far up the mountain as possible? Such questions begin addressing the relationship of goals to structure.

The Mount Everest climb of 1985 pursued as its objective an expeditionary siege. This team had as its objective getting one member of the team to the top of the mountain. As such, its entire structure and design was intended to produce such an outcome. Some of the members were to act as a support group in order to get the one or two strongest members to the summit. Team member George McLeod recalled that this was not quite the way the climb worked out:

> When you go to a mountain like Mount Everest, the idea is not to get worn out—so that you will still have something left for the rest of the climb. An expedition like that takes three months. You're living in a very threatening, hostile situation. Base camp, for example, was at 17,800 feet, and a lot of people get mountain sickness at about 14,000 feet.
>
> So here you have 20 climbers fresh, ready, and willing to go up the mountain. What begins to happen, however, is that a few people are being used on such a strong daily basis that they fade within a month. Unfortunately, for the first portion of the climb we used some of the best climbers we had, which shouldn't have happened. Instead, we should have shared responsibilities more equally.
>
> I think we should have sat down as a group, which we seldom did, and discussed how we were going to make this happen . . . . We didn't take the summit. But we got to 28,200 feet which was only 800 feet from the top. There were a lot of flaws in the group in terms of getting together and forming a team . . . . It was quite shattering to see all kinds of things falling apart.

On the other hand, the first women's team to be invited to climb Mount Kongur in China identified a slightly different goal and a structure that was correspondingly suited to achieving the goal. Pat Dillingham, a member of the Mount Kongur expedition, defined the goal of the climb as "much more consensus-based, such that the goal was not to get someone on top but rather to get as many people as high on the mountain as we could." Dillingham went on to describe the structural design of the team that the members felt made the most sense.

The type of climb we did is called an alpine climb, as opposed to what George McLeod was involved in on Mount Everest, which was an expeditionary siege style of climb. The alpine means that it was just the nine of us in charge of getting ourselves as high as we could on the mountain and carrying our own loads, as opposed to using 100 to 200 Sherpas, the support groups, and everybody else who's involved with a siege-style expedition. The alpine style is much more defined—and definitely the way mountaineering is going right now. In the old siege style, you end up taking the picnic table, chairs, barbecues, and everything else. The alpine style of climbing involves just taking the essentials. It's much easier for the alpine to have all team members with the same objective: "Let's get to the top or as high as we can."

Unequivocally, teams should be designed around the results to be achieved, rather than around any preexisting or extraneous circumstances. For a structure to be functional and useful, it must be established in such a way that individual and combined efforts always lead toward the desired goal. As such, the first judgment to be made must focus on the broad, or overall objective of a team. Our findings indicate that there are three broad objectives which, in turn, require three different structural emphases.

THREE BASIC STRUCTURES

Teams are capable of having a number of alternative structures. An analysis of the teams in our investigation strongly suggests that the best starting point for determining the appropriate structure of a team is to answer the following question: At the broadest level, what should be the result—or objective—of our collective effort? Our analysis of the responses to that question indicates that there are three basic broad team objectives, leading to the formation of three types of teams (see Table 3.1): (1) problem resolution, (2) creative, and (3) tactical.

1. Problem-Resolution Teams

The first broad team objective we identified from our interviews was ". . . to resolve problems on an ongoing basis." When this is the broad purpose of the collective team effort, the most important and necessary feature of the team is TRUST. Each member of the team

TABLE 3.1
Basic Structures

Broad Objective	Dominant Feature	Process Emphasis	Examples
1. Problem resolution	Trust	Focus on issues	• American Leadership Forum • Centers for Disease Control
2. Creative	Autonomy	Explore possibilities and alternatives	• IBM PC team • McDonald's Chicken McNugget team
3. Tactical	Clarity	Directive Highly focused tasks Role clarity Well-defined operational standards Accuracy	• Cardiac Surgery • USS *Kitty Hawk* Crew

must expect and believe that interactions among members will be truthful and embody a high degree of integrity. Each member must believe that the team will be fairly consistent and mature in its approach to dealing with problems. And, each member must believe and expect that every member will be valued and treated with respect. Consider the following two examples of problem-resolution teams: The American Leadership Forum and epidemiology teams at the Centers for Disease Control.

AMERICAN LEADERSHIP FORUM

Joe Jaworski, a successful trial attorney in the Houston area, described the feelings he had in the mid-1970s that led to his founding of the American Leadership Forum (ALF).

Perspectives began changing in the '70s. People around age 40 were basically discouraged from stepping out and leading in the community, region, or nationally. As a result, a sort of civic cynicism was growing up.

I began feeling all of those things in the mid-'70s. Watergate had just finished, and my dad [Leon Jaworski] had been deeply involved, and it touched me deeply as well. I had rightly or wrongly understood that "they" were in charge out there in Washington, or elsewhere, and everything was okay. All we had to do was our little piece of it. This was obviously totally wrong, and the Watergate experience pulled me up sharply and made me really begin thinking about how we each need to contribute, or we are in real trouble.

I went off to London for three years because I had committed to building our firm's office there. When you move away from it all, you see things more clearly.

I really put this whole leadership issue together in my mind about 1975. By 1980, everybody was writing about it, and I had this plan for American Leadership Forum. I felt like the timing was right—Russians had marched on Afghanistan; Carter had the Iranian crisis; economic problems were generating massive social problems. *Time* magazine did a special issue on the leadership gap, as did *Newsweek* and *U.S. News*. I felt a personal need to try and do something.

The ultimate vision was to put in each community a smaller community of strengthened leaders who had shared perspectives about making that place a better place to live—people who would literally begin taking responsibility for what happened in that community.

Consistent with Joe Jaworski's objective of placing leadership back in the hands of community members was the structure he designed for building community teams. The basic structure of each team places a heavy emphasis on process skills—the manner in which people choose to relate to one another. It was apparent to Jaworski early on that most community problems go unresolved because the people addressing them often engage in behaviors that produce distrust: hidden agendas, self-vested interests, favors for special constituencies.

Jaworski's strategy was simple, insightful, and twofold. First, ALF selects about 20 people within a community who do not share a history of dealing at length with one another. The wisdom of this approach resides in the fact that people who have not dealt with one another before have not had an opportunity to formulate impressions of one another that might get in the way of problem-solving. The reality of conflict—as we are all aware—is that when the conflict is over, the parties involved usually share in a brief powerful history that can leave negative impressions about the other party. By initiating new interaction patterns, Jaworski's approach circumvented most of this type of entanglement.

Second, Jaworski took the 20 "strangers" and made their first experience with one another an experience that would build trust. This was accomplished by putting the group through an outdoor adventure training experience. Through such experiences as rock climbing, rappelling down cliffs, and group problem-solving, the team learns to work together. Then the team is guided through individual and group exercises that cause members to reflect upon their ability to work together as a team. Once group members develop a strong bond of trust, they envision and plan a collaborative project directed toward improving their community.

As can be seen, the basic strategy for structuring teams within American Leadership Forum revolves around processes that heavily emphasize building trust and working relationships with the ultimate objective of solving problems.

CENTERS FOR DISEASE CONTROL

The goal of epidemiology is to stop the transmission of disease as soon as possible and then study that disease and its transmission. Epidemiology is the science of mathematics applied to medicine. It is an investigative effort to determine the "rate" of disease transmission

within given populations of people. Epidemiologists attempt to discover the right numerators and denominators helpful in calculating
the differences in rates of transmission for populations being compared.

Epidemiology is concerned with fact-based decisions. Critical to
this process is the construction of the best available data base from
which to make judgments. Consider the following case described by
Dr. Michael D. Gregg, deputy director of epidemiology programs for
the Centers for Disease Control:

> In 1955, the CDC took the responsibility of evaluating the polio vac-
> cine developed by Jonas Salk, and there was a fair amount of encour-
> agement about its licensing. It was expected to save millions of lives,
> and little kids would no longer be crippled.
>
> Alex Langmuir, who was then the chief epidemiologist at CDC and
> the eventual team leader in evaluating the polio vaccine, tells the fol-
> lowing prescient story: In late 1954, six vaccine manufacturers met with
> the Division of Biological Standards, with Jonas Salk, and a number of
> other people. Some of them had been having problems with inactiva-
> tion of the virus during the process of vaccine manufacture. While one
> of the manufacturers was explaining that his company had been more
> efficient and successful at inactivating the virus, a representative from
> one of the other manufacturers had a telephone call, left the room, and
> came back after the discussion on inactivating the virus was over. . . .
>
> Within two weeks after the beginning of the nationwide vaccination
> program, in April 1955 CDC began to get reports of polio. What was
> significant was that these children had received the vaccine six to eight
> days earlier and had developed polio, almost invariably, in the arm or
> the leg where they had received the shot.
>
> Within 48 hours of the reports of only six polio cases in children,
> Alex Langmuir and CDC were able to tell the Surgeon General two
> things: one, the vaccine contaminated with live virus was manufactured
> by the laboratory whose representative took the phone call during the
> discussion on inactivating the virus; and two, the message that the
> vaccination program could be continued with the remaining uncontami-
> nated lots.
>
> Both of those messages were very important. The first is the old
> physician's motto, "Do no harm." Get the contaminated lots off the
> market so we don't produce any more disease. But what is equally
> important is not to damn by association the five other manufacturers
> who are making polio vaccine—continue the vaccination program be-
> cause we've got a big polio season likely to come up. . . .

In any kind of team effort. you've got to be sure that everybody hears what everybody else has to say. There's an obligation of communication. There's an obligation of almost even a checklist. Everybody has to know pretty much everything if they want to be a successful group of people moving forward on any kind of project.

While some investigations and corresponding judgments are made directly by the Centers for Disease Control, it would be impossible for the 600 to 1,000 epidemics identified yearly in the United States to be handled directly on a centralized basis. Consequently, the field of epidemiology is organized in a decentralized structure. While there are strong centralized resources provided by the CDC, state and local epidemiologists are critical to the process. According to Dr. Lyle Conrad, director of Field Operations at CDC:

It comes back to the roles of all these people on these teams. The political heat is up first and hottest at the local level because that's where the problems are. However, seldom do local health departments have the resources to deal with all the possible problems they encounter. Rather, the most expeditious use of money means having the ability to recognize the problem and then to call for help.

The first place they call is their state, because that health officer and that state epidemiologist are bound by their laws to respond to those problems. Their response can only be one of two: They can respond directly from their own staff and deal with the problem by sending their own epidemiologists, lab support, or general field workers. Or, they can call CDC or a university and get assistance.

The teams in epidemiology in the U.S., by and large, are no bigger than two or three people. Each one is put together, sort of planned out a little bit, but you take advantage of who's available, whose territory you're in, who wants to work on it, and then who's available from the career staff to back them up and to advise them.

Sometimes the epidemics take very little time and limited data to assess and control, such as a cholera outbreak in Louisiana. According to Dr. Conrad, "We hadn't had any cholera in this country for more than 100 years. With cholera, you die of dehydration if the doctors don't recognize you have it. It was one of the cases in Louisiana that tipped them off—a man who had 50 stools a day."

Other cases, however, are not as easy to resolve. Dr. Michael Gregg discussed one rather interesting case:

This was a fascinating epidemic of salmonellosis. a bacterial disease that gives you diarrhea. fever. and cramps. There were about 750 cases—a big. big outbreak that occurred in a little town in Oregon called The Dalles.

We sent one of our first-year trainees to The Dalles to work on the epidemic. As soon as he got in. he realized that this was a huge outbreak, and one person—particularly a young. inexperienced epidemiologist—really wasn't going to be able to handle 750 cases. So. we sent in another epidemiologist to help him. They did a lot of work for about two weeks. but they didn't have an answer. It looked like a common-source outbreak—a lot of people becoming ill very rapidly over a relatively short period of time. Then it was decided to bring in the big guns from the CDC in Atlanta.

Approximately two months went by. which is too long for us. The only conclusion that had been drawn from the data was that there were 10 simultaneous outbreaks of salmonella associated with 10 different restaurants in The Dalles. Yet everyone felt that there was a common source associated with each of the salad bars in those restaurants. and that there was a statistical association with eating in the salad bar in all 10 restaurants. Still. we hadn't found the source of the problem—the mayonnaise. or the blue cheese. or the distributor who brings vegetables into The Dalles. etc. We knew we were not going to have 10 simultaneous outbreaks occurring in 10 different restaurants without there being a common source that is related to all of them. Yet there was no reasonable epidemiological explanation. It wasn't until we began looking outside our traditional data base that we found the answer.

We found out relatively late in the investigation that the community had been having an ongoing fight with a religious sect. There had been accusations that this religious sect had poisoned the food—causing the outbreak. I knew about this; we all knew about this; but we focused our attention on a nonmanmade phenomenon. After all. 99.9999% of what we do has no legal connotations. We don't look at humans doing something to produce disease. We look at natural. rare events that get together to produce outbreaks like this.

Roughly a year after the epidemic. the FBI discovered that this religious sect had bought salmonella organisms from a biological supply company on the East Coast. It was the exact serotype that caused the epidemic. Ultimately. the leader of this sect admitted that they had poisoned the salad bars.

Clearly. the real challenge for the Centers for Disease Control is to gather data as close to the problem as possible. By its very nature, this effort implies a decentralized structure. As with many problems, however, the balance between closeness to the problem and the availability of necessary resources depends on the presence of—and intervention by—a centralized body of expertise. It is this structural configuration that allows for the quickest response to a problem, the most thorough investigative effort, the creation of a data-based decision-making process, and the realization of economies of scale in managing resources and expertise. Those who have firsthand knowledge of and experience with the problem and those who command technical and supporting resources must be able to surface, discuss, and resolve the issues that lead to the problem's solution.

The primary consideration for a team whose objective is problem resolution and whose necessary feature is trust is a process that focuses on issues, rather than on predetermined positions or conclusions. The quickest way to neuter a problem-resolution team is for individual members to become fixated on solutions before identifying and understanding the critical issues contained in the problem. After all, problem-resolution teams, such as the American Leadership Forum teams, or the Centers for Disease Control, or any executive management team, are really an effort to allow sound judgment to grow out of a careful, investigative, and mutually-informing process.

2. Creative Teams

A second response to the question regarding the broad objective of a team is "to create something." When the broad objective of the team emphasizes creativity, then a necessary feature of the structure of the team is AUTONOMY. The process focus for the creative team is that of exploring possibilities and alternatives. Creativity, by definition, is the abandonment of normative thinking. Therefore, for a creative team to function, it is necessary to have autonomy from systems and procedures, as well as to create an atmosphere in which ideas do not become prematurely quashed. Consider, for example, the IBM PC team and the Chicken McNugget team.

IBM PC TEAM

The seemingly "overnight success" of the IBM PC was actually prefaced by years of groundwork and careful planning. According to Larry Rojas, the technical planning manager for the personal computer project, the PC was really the last of a long line of machines, not all of which were successful. But, as Rojas points out, the way the project team was structured played just as significant a role in the successful creation of the PC as did its technological lineage.

The structure of the PC project team contained several features that oriented the efforts of team members toward the desired results.

- The PC team was removed from the inner workings of the organization. Rather than requiring the team to work in proximity to the Armonk, New York headquarters, the team was physically located in Boca Raton, Florida, where it managed itself almost autonomously. Members from other parts of the organization were refused visiting rights. As Rojas pointed out: "We were a totally self-contained organization, much like a small business. The only thing we needed was money and management approval. As a matter of fact, we would discuss it in those terms."
- The team remained insulated from the rest of the organization through a carefully prescribed communication strategy. Every two months the project leader, the late Don Estridge, would take his technical planning manager (Larry Rojas) and a few select people "up north" to spend two weeks at the Armonk headquarters informing key constituencies of the status of the project and resolving important issues. Key constituencies consisted of three specific points of contact within the organization: pricing, quality assurance, and forecasting. Several presentations were also made to other appropriate groups of people. As Larry Rojas recalls: "During one of those two-week stretches, we kept track of the number of presentations that were made. On this one occasion, there were 56. This process was repeated every two months."
- External communication to the rest of the corporation was fairly formal, and internal communication did contain a formal skeletal structure, such as staff meetings and Monday morning planning meetings. The thrust of the internal communication, however, was informal interactions. According to Rojas, the atmosphere tended more toward what he called "copy machine management," where brief informal meetings were held as needed, even among varying levels within the PC organization. The informality extended to "Saturday morning playtime," when employees were encouraged to use the boxes and related software to teach themselves, and even family members, all about PCs.

CHICKEN MCNUGGET PROJECT

"The project was finally copied. The first one to copy the project was Kentucky Fried Chicken. I thought that was the absolute form of flattery!" Such were the words of E.J. (Bud) Sweeney. In the fall of 1979, Bud Sweeney was asked by McDonald's Corporation to head up a new project to attempt to bring bits of batter-covered chicken to the marketplace. Until then, fast food chicken consisted of primary parts—thighs, legs, breasts, wings. According to Sweeney:

> The chairman of the board of McDonald's, Fred Turner, was the progenitor of this project—to create battered pieces of chicken meat, deboned, that you would dip into sauces—finger food. Going through the regular channels and management layers, the product development department had selected a supplier and developed the product as close as they were able and put it in a small test market in two stores in Indianapolis. That's where I came in.

When Bud Sweeney accepted responsibility for the project, the product was in two stores, and it was failing. After visiting the two test markets, Sweeney fired the supplier and started from zero. He picked another supplier who was not a "chicken person." Actually it was one of McDonald's largest meat suppliers, who had a small meat-processing plant in Nashville, Tennessee. As Sweeney recalled:

> We knew that there were bricks and mortar and people there so we figured we could get everything out and use that facility for our hands-on research and development. We knew what our ultimate goal was: to simulate and then cut chicken meat, which was to be dipped in batter. However, it was to be done with all the refined production equipment available in today's marketplace.

The structure of the project team, for what eventually became known as Chicken McNugget, was relatively simple. Three primary members composed the "swat team." The team name reminded its members that their objective was to get something done quickly. They were to develop a product, test it, and decide whether they had something worthwhile. The team functioned completely autonomously, reporting the results directly to Fred Turner.

The project leader, Sweeney, was largely responsible for the design of the team. His experience with product development suggested to him that there was a good chance this project would fail if it were required to grow within the traditional organization structure. Sweeney commented:

Over the years. I've seen so many projects go dry at the corporate level because of layers of insulated bureaucracy. This one was fairly intense. The goal was simple.

I've seen some good products never make it because they displease various levels of management. With so many obstacles, they never make the breakthrough to test. I refused the project initially. Then the chairman put his nose next to mine and told me I'd become a poor listener.

Fred Turner had been somewhat "agnostic" regarding new products. Show me. Prove it to me. Double it. On this particular one, however. I saw a sparkle in his eye. And, truthfully, what he had seen up to that point wasn't that great a trial product. It was, however, a great concept.

I told him I'd take the project if I could put together the team and report to no one. I would give him the results, but I would be the ultimate team leader. Also, I would handpick my team from employees of his corporation. It was fairly ad hoc.

Not unlike the IBM PC team, the McNugget team needed breathing room within a large corporate structure in order to remain focused on the result to be achieved rather than on other organizational considerations. The autonomous structure of the swat team became the necessary framework for the team to function successfully.

Equally important was the decision-making process established by the three primary swat team members. Bud Sweeney was swat one. Swat two was McDonald's corporate director of quality assurance. Swat three was a manager who was third or fourth in command of the product development department. There were some other members who would come and go, but it was the three primary members who would resolve issues and make decisions.

The process for doing so was fairly simple. Each of the three team members had one third of the vote. All decisions were made by two of the three primary members favoring a specific resolution. This forced a decision-making process that was swift and required immediate explanation when a vote was taken. As Sweeney noted, "We made our greatest progress when we were nose to nose."

A simple structure: three primary players; a minimal number of constraints imposed by the existing corporate structure; available resources; and an agreed-upon decision-making process that forced communication and speedy resolutions. The results of the team's work are perhaps the best testimony for the team formula used. The first test markets—about 16 stores—were opened on March 5, 1980, six months after the project began. The test markets were expanded in increments of thousands of stores, and the product went system-wide in the summer of 1983.

Just as with the IBM PC team, which separated itself from IBM's headquarters, or McDonald's Chicken McNugget project, which consisted of a three-man team reporting directly to the chairman, creative teams must be given room to breathe. To be successful, the creative team must be set free of the control and potential rigidity associated with the more traditional organizational structure.

3. Tactical Teams

The third broad team objective we identified was " . . . to execute a well-defined plan." This broad-brushed objective is most notably characterized by CLARITY. For tactical teams to be successful, there must be high task clarity and unambiguous role definition. Consider the examples of a cardiac surgical team and the crew of an aircraft carrier. The success of each of these teams depends upon a high degree of responsiveness from team members, a high degree of clarity in terms of who does what, and a clear set of performance standards.

CARDIAC SURGERY TEAMS

Dr. Don Wukasch spent nine years as a cardiac surgeon on the Michael DeBakey surgical team and 10 years on the Denton Cooley team. With 10 open-heart surgeries occurring simultaneously and each surgical procedure taking about three hours, these high performance surgical teams were ultimately conducting 30 to 40 surgical procedures a day.

During his 19 years as a cardiac surgeon, Dr. Wukasch experienced several instances of outstanding team performance, perhaps best exemplified by the following two events.

We were beginning an emergency operation for a patient with a ruptured spleen. When we opened the abdomen, the blood just gushed out. We had about three or four seconds to get in there and clamp the artery before she would bleed to death. Just as we opened her, the lights went out. A hurricane was hitting, and the power went off. We only had several seconds before it was completely dark—no lights, no windows.

I didn't know then that they had flashlights hanging in the corners, but the nurses apparently did. Within three seconds we had lights, and we were back in action. That's what real professionalism is.

The same thing happened at the Texas Heart Institute. A hurricane again—the power went out, and the patient was on the heart-lung machine. When the power goes off, the heart-lung machine goes off. You have about a minute or two before the patient starts to die. I didn't know we had them, but there are hand cranks under each heart-lung machine. The team started cranking, and within 15 seconds we were going at normal. Here again, no panic, just a smooth operation. That's real professionalism. That's a high-performance team.

Well, everyone learns their job. I didn't know that the infusion team had been practicing doing the hand crank, but apparently that's part of their training. They all trained on their own individual components. It's fun being part of the team when everyone does their part.

The teams that Dr. Wukasch observed firsthand were organized and structured to achieve a high degree of role clarity. Each task was clearly focused and accompanied by a well-defined operational standard.

USS KITTY HAWK CREW

Picture yourself as the captain of a large ship with the following managerial responsibilities: You have a staff of 5,000 people—about two thirds of whom are teenagers. Your cargo includes dozens of fighter planes and an unimaginable amount of nuclear explosives. You are bouncing around in the ocean at approximately 30 knots, and you're open for business 24 hours a day.

Such were the responsibilities of Rear Admiral Ned Hogan, former commander of the USS *Kitty Hawk*. As defined by Admiral Hogan, the objective in managing the USS *Kitty Hawk* is "execution without problems!" The situation calls for clarity of responsibilities and accountabilities. Everyone must understand his job and how that job relates to the defined mission of the ship. Everyone must understand that the ship must always be ready; be able to go from point A to point B; and execute the schedule—whether that schedule is launching airplanes, recovering them, conducting a port visit in a proper way as ambassadors of goodwill, or upholding the integrity and safety of the United States during a military confrontation.

Much like cardiac surgical teams, each operational procedure of the USS *Kitty Hawk* must be well-defined; each task must be highly focused and very specific; the standards of excellence must be clear to everyone; and ways of measuring success or failure must be available to and understood by the entire team.

The team whose broad objective is tactical must begin with clear definitions—both of the overall task and of each task that supports it. There must be role clarity in terms of who performs each task, and each task must be accompanied by a well-defined set of operational standards. Teams emphasizing execution are best served by a structure and corresponding processes that are highly directive—specifying WHO, WHAT, WHEN, WHERE, WHY, and HOW.

FOUR NECESSARY FEATURES OF TEAM STRUCTURE

Once the team structure has been framed according to its broadest objective—problem-solving, creativity, or tactical execution—it becomes possible to emphasize the characteristics that our research suggests are structural properties of effective teams. For problem-solving teams, the structure promotes *trust*; for creativity teams, the structure allows for *autonomy*; and for tactical teams, the structure reinforces *clarity*.

Beyond these structural variations, we also found four design features that seemed to characterize effectively functioning teams in general: (1) clear roles and accountabilities; (2) an effective communication system; (3) methods for monitoring individual performance and providing feedback; and (4) an emphasis on fact-based judgments. The degree of emphasis of these features varied with the team objectives.

1. Clear Roles and Accountabilities

Each member's relationship to the team must be defined in terms of the role to be assumed and the results the role is to produce. Eventually, any team effort boils down to the assumption of individual responsibilities and accountabilities.

Think back to the surgical team discussed earlier. Successful heart surgery is clearly a team effort, but the team's success is only as good as the collective performances by each individual. In short, each member of any successful team must understand at the outset what he or she will be held accountable for and measured against in terms of performance.

This first feature of a results-driven structure is absolutely essential to team success. Without clear roles and accountabilities, all efforts become random and haphazard—perhaps even failing as in the flash-flood example cited earlier in this chapter. It follows that the team is unable to systematize its efforts in such a way that it can repeat its performance and even raise the standards bar one notch higher. Our research strongly suggests that EVERYONE IS ACCOUNTABLE ALL THE TIME on successful teams.

2. An Effective Communication System

The sample of teams we interviewed yielded a very clear set of variables related to an effective communication system. *The first of these variables focuses on information that is easily accessible.* Captain William Bauman, one of the writers of the official report on the results of the Challenger disaster investigation, pointed out that there were work areas of information, written and pictorial, which were made available to all members of the investigation team. It was felt that only through information that was easily accessible to all investigators could the problem that resulted in the explosion of the Challenger space shuttle be identified.

Second, the information that is available must emerge from credible sources. The quality of a decision is directly related to the accuracy of the information upon which that decision was based. And the team's confidence in the sources of valid information determines its willingness to engage in active or bold decision-making. This feature is so basic to team effectiveness that it is hard to imagine an effectively functioning team which does not place high value on credible sources of information.

Third, there must be opportunities for team members to raise issues not on the formal agenda. This necessary feature of successful teams emerged as a common thread throughout the team interviews we conducted. The IBM PC team encouraged Saturday morning playtime for more informal interaction. Ruth Rothstein, CEO of Mt. Sinai Hospital in Chicago, discussed the importance of providing opportunities for teams to meet socially or informally. Duke Drake, who served as CEO of Dun and Bradstreet Corporation for 10 years, talked about taking his key management team to a ranch in Arizona, where there were no phones in the rooms, where you could see fifty miles in every direction, where you could discuss long-range plans in a mind-expanding environment and develop friendships around the campfire at night—or on the back of a horse. Joe Madden, manager of the Small ICBM (Midgetman) programs at Boeing, which include the Hard Mobile Launcher and the Weapon Control System, referred to these opportunities as "informal chat time."

However this phenomenon is thought of, the necessary element that emerged from our research was the importance of providing team members with *opportunities* to discuss team issues in a relaxed environment—an environment where titles and positions in the organization mean less than they normally do, where size of offices is not part of the territory, and where the formality of business suits is replaced by shirt-sleeved discussions.

Fourth, an effective communication system must possess methods for documenting issues raised and decisions made. The approved criteria for the design decisions made by the 747 team are contained in the "Design Objectives and Criteria Book." This book contains the accumulated knowledge from issues raised and decisions made during the construction of consecutive airplane projects. The accuracy of this record and its value is best exemplified by Boeing's refusal to accept $100 million from the Soviet government for a copy of the book on the 747. Similarly, the importance of good documentation may be seen in the Challenger investigation team's use of a documentation system developed by the Justice Department. There were 6,000 people who participated directly or indirectly on the Challenger team, generating massive amounts of information that had to be managed accurately and cross-referenced for ease of access.

Whatever the system used for documenting issues raised and decisions made, the key ingredient is the discipline required to capture accurately the decisions made by a team on an ongoing basis. Keeping an accurate record of the team's actions and decisions prevents wasteful duplication of effort and reduces confusion.

3. Monitoring Individual Performance and Providing Feedback

Overcoming deficiencies requires checks and balances, both at a systems level—such as testing products to see how they work under various conditions—and at a level of individual performance of each person on the team.

There is an abundance of literature on performance appraisal systems and methods for evaluating individual contributions. Suffice it to say that without the accurate appraisal of an individual's performance, several other outcomes begin to weaken. Without knowing an individual's performance, it becomes impossible to determine, with any sense of accuracy and equity, how the individual should be rewarded, what the individual's development needs are, and what increased or further responsibilities this individual might assume in the future.

4. Fact-Based Judgments

The last structural feature that emerged from the teams we studied accentuates the need for objective and factual data as a basis for sound decision-making. Of course, different types of fact bases serve different needs. The Centers for Disease Control, for example, uses the case-control study method in which facts are based upon the mathematical frequencies of a numerator (number of cases) over a denominator (relevant population). Other facts, however, may be established by demonstrating whether something is possible, such as the creation of a new product. Whatever the data base, it is important to base decisions on sound facts and to make sure that facts are interpreted without the harness of predisposition.

In summary, there are two primary considerations concerning effective team structures. The first requires a determination of the broad objective to be achieved by the team. This broad objective is likely to fit one of three possible types: problem resolution, creativity, or tactical execution. Each of these broad objectives implies a different structural emphasis: trust, autonomy, or clarity.

The second consideration in determining an effective team structure focuses on those four features that appear to be common success factors in the design of an effective team: (1) clear roles and accountabilities, (2) an effective communication system, (3) monitoring performance and providing feedback, (4) fact-based decision-making. The systems associated with each of these four features become the framework through which the clear, elevating goal can be achieved.

4

Competent Team Members

When asked to cite factors that would account for the success of a team, interviewees in our sample consistently said it was imperative to select the right people. All too often, people are chosen as team members for the wrong reasons. "Harry should be on the team because he's interested in the topic." Or, "Bill's feelings would be hurt if he were left off." Or, "Mary should be included because she reports to Bill." These may be important considerations, but they don't necessarily lead to successful teams. Instead, what should be paramount is selecting people who are best equipped to achieve the team's objective. Consider the subtle but apparent selection differences in the following three examples.

Example 1: The 1966 Notre Dame National Championship Football Team. It's no coincidence that 19 of the 21 players who completed the season were subsequently drafted by the pros. Now a successful business executive, Tom Quinn was a sophomore defensive back on the 1966 championship team. As Quinn recalled, "We had some awesome talent on the team: players like Nick Eddy, Alan Page, Jim Seymour, Terry Hanratty, Kevin Hardy, and Jim Lynch. Their qualities as people and their abilities as players accounted for much of the uniqueness and excellence of that team."

Wide receiver Jim Seymour was the second half of the Hanratty/Seymour equation, perhaps best remembered for their game against Purdue, a team which at that time was quarterbacked by Bob Griese. During that game, Terry Hanratty and Jim Seymour teamed up for 13 completed passes, three of which were for touchdowns. It was that game that landed Hanratty and Seymour on the cover of *Time* magazine.

During our interview with Jim Seymour, he referred to the "Iron Belt Strip." Apparently, Lou Holtz, as the new head coach of Notre Dame, talked to Ara Parseghian and several of his former assistants to try and identify a selection pattern that may have accounted for the talent on Parseghian's teams. They actually identified a geographical strip of the United States where most of the starters came from during Parseghian's 11 years as head coach. According to Seymour, "It's a strip that starts in Pennsylvania and comes across Ohio, Illinois, and Michigan. A few guys were from the Los Angeles area; one or two out of Texas. However, the majority of them were from the Iron Belt."

Seymour emphasized the fact that it wasn't merely skill at the game of football that made the Iron Belt a rich source of talent for Parseghian's teams:

> The Iron Belt produced high school football players who possessed a certain personal characteristic. The parents of these kids came up the hard way. They believe that if you want to succeed in life you have to work real hard. That's how the parents approached it, and that's how they raised their kids. When you put talent alongside a willingness to work real hard, that's a tough combination to beat.

Example 2: Field epidemiologists for the Centers for Disease Control. Selection criteria for field epidemiologists at the CDC must take into account the need for team members to work independently as investigators in their assigned state. According to Dr. Lyle Conrad, director of Field Operations, and Dr. Michael Gregg, acting deputy director of the Epidemiology Program Office, the field epidemiologist must possess a well-defined set of characteristics.

The epidemiologist must be (1) technically competent, which includes being analytically bright enough to take problems apart from an investigative standpoint; (2) friendly and outgoing, able to get along with others; (3) politically astute, knowing when to lead and when not to; (4) willing to subordinate his or her own personal interests in favor of the overall objective of the investigation; (5) willing to spend an inordinate amount of time sifting through the available facts; (6) imaginative, so that he or she will ask "unusual" questions of the data; (7) honest and possess integrity in interpreting the data accurately; (8) interested in doing things that are challenging and different. As Dr. Conrad put it, "We never put them back where they came from. They always get assigned somewhere else."

The thrust of the challenge in selecting epidemiologists, then, is to find someone who is analytically disciplined, while at the same time interpersonally adroit and capable of working collaboratively with different state agencies and local authorities. Obviously, the selection of epidemiologists would be a monumental challenge even given a large pool of talent. The problem, however, is geometrically complicated by the fact that there are far more epidemics than epidemiologists to study them. According to Dr. Conrad:

> I was once given an estimate that 3,500 outbreaks or problems occur in the U.S. each year. We look at anywhere from 600 to 1,000 depending on how many people we have on duty. Last year, we did 650 outbreaks with 45 people. Our country is short at least 1,000, maybe 2,000, trained epidemiologists.

Given this lack of balance between supply and demand, it would be easy to ignore the selection criteria. But given the importance of the work it does, the CDC encourages a very careful selection process.

Example 3: The Rogers Commission. Generally regarded as one of the finest investigative teams in recent history, the Rogers Commission not only determined the cause of the space shuttle Challenger disaster, but also those factors that contributed to it. The success of the Rogers Commision is believed to be directly related to the quality of people, both the thirteen Commissioners and the supporting staff who were on that team.

Lieutenant Colonel Thomas Reinhardt was drawn from the White House staff to be the Commission's executive secretary. He identified the criteria used for selecting people for the Rogers Commission. Prospective staff members had to (1) have the technical knowledge, skills, and relevant background to unravel why the disaster occurred; (2) be honest and trustworthy and not allow any self-vested interests or outside constituencies to have a bearing on the facts gathered; (3) be willing to work hard and invest long hours in order to satisfy President Reagan's request that the project be brought to a conclusion within 120 days; (4) care about the tragic human side of the disaster; (5) understand that the future of the United States manned space flight program was at stake; (6) recognize that the National Aeronautics and Space Administration is a unique national asset and that therefore only the highest standards would be accepted in reaching the objectives of the project.

Since there were about 6,000 people who worked on the actual space shuttle accident analysis, and a 120-day deadline, much depended on the ability of the Commission to keep to the task at hand.

Captain William Bauman, one of the authors of the final report, pointed out:

> Some of those folks are heavyweight thinkers. Others are not only
> heavyweight thinkers, but also very skilled administrators. It was an
> excellent team effort, and leadership was exceptional. William Rogers
> was always on focus; Alton Keel was always on focus.

TWO TYPES OF COMPETENCIES

What is a competent team member? According to our interviewees, what matters most is selecting members who possess (1) the necessary technical skills and abilities to achieve the desired objective, and (2) the personal characteristics required to achieve excellence while working well with others. While technical skills are a bit easier to identify, the best teams are composed with a selection strategy that attempts to capture both qualities.

Technical competencies are the minimal requirement on any team. They refer to the substantive knowledge, skills, and abilities related to the team's objective. They are what a team member must know and be able to do well in order to have a reasonable chance of achieving the team's objective.

To say that different teams require different technical competencies is to comment on the obvious. The real trick, according to our research, is first to know what the *critical technical skills* are, and second to know what the necessary *balance* of those skills should be on any given team. As might be expected, each team objective presents its own unique set of technical challenges.

One unique criterion for selecting members of teams for the General Accounting Office of the government (GAO)—one primary responsibility of which is to provide information to Congress from which sound decisions can be made—is oral communications skills. According to Charles Bowsher, Comptroller General for the United States and head of the GAO, one of the "critical" technical skills is the ability to communicate orally, and particularly to be an effective witness before a congressional committee. Therefore, this skill is emphasized at all levels in GAO, and a major effort is made to train people in oral communication. As Bowsher pointed out, "An impor-

tant part of our human resources development effort is to build a
senior staff, every member of which possesses this skill."

For Linda Alvarado, CEO of Alvarado Construction, it's important to have a balance between the "nuts and bolts types" and those
individuals who are capable of being creative and conceptual. According to Alvarado, in the construction business it's important to have
the "big picture" people who can see the conceptual side of a project
and know when major changes are necessary. This needs to be balanced, however, by people who are at the job site supervising the
very detail-oriented portions of the work. Both are necessary members of a good project team.

The level and composition of technical skills are also important
issues in mountain climbing, but with a slightly different focus. Mountain climber and climbing instructor Pat Dillingham emphasized team
members' skill comparability. "If the skill level is radically different,
then trust is compromised. That leads to all kinds of problems that
are not good for teams. Technical competency is important because
the consequences are so life-threatening."

Personal competencies refer to the qualities, skills, and abilities
necessary for the individual team members to identify, address, and
resolve issues. It is personal competencies that allow people to function as a team. The types of individuals, their qualities as people,
the talents they bring with them, and their abilities to work together
toward a common objective are critical determinants of team success. Once again, we have found that teams that achieve excellence
are able to identify and raise all types of issues related to the team's
objective, discuss these issues in a fact-based way, and eventually
arrive at resolutions that emerge from the collaborative effort.
These process capabilities determine the internal performance of a
team. The extent to which they are present will directly impact team
success.

Although personal competency requirements may vary from team
to team, there are some "similar" characteristics that begin to emerge
from our data. The important thing to remember is that successful
teams take the time to identify and promote the required personal
characteristics.

Consider, for example, McDonald's Chicken McNugget team. Bud
Sweeney, the team leader, told us he specifically looked for people
who were "intelligent, creative, tenacious, and a bit of a maverick—

willing to buck the system and not be bound by traditional thinking and reporting relationships." This cluster of personal characteristics, according to Sweeney, contributed significantly to bringing the McNugget product to market within six months.

Slightly different from the well-defined project team is the ongoing executive management team. Unlike a project team, which typically focuses on a single objective, ongoing management teams are a bit more diffused as they tackle a wider range of problem-solving activities. Consider the personal characteristics emphasized as selection standards for the following three executive management teams: Dun and Bradstreet, Emerson Electric, and Baxter International.

As chairman and CEO for 10 years, Harrington (Duke) Drake has been a principal architect of Dun and Bradstreet. According to Drake, when he took over as chairman in 1975 his first priority was to build a senior management team. His selection standards for senior executives consisted of five principles:

> First I looked for bright people. Not much can be accomplished if people aren't bright thinkers. However, I also wanted people who were street-smart and able to read the tea leaves. Third, I wanted boy scouts. Fourth, they had to be hard workers—no shortcuts. And last, no politicians.

As a final note regarding competent team members, Drake offered the following observation. "It's equally important to eliminate the mediocre people. When you put talent in charge of an organization, the morale goes up."

Emerson Electric's chairman, Charles F. Knight, described in a very deliberate fashion the criteria for selecting members of an executive management team: "They must have a commitment to success. That's where it all starts. They must have an ability to deal with people. There must be a sense of urgency to make something happen. There has to be an ability to set priorities; to be able to think clearly about a problem; to be fair with people; and a willingness to set high standards and demand them of others."

Similarly, Baxter International, under the direction of chairman and CEO Vernon R. Loucks, has identified and articulated those factors that appear to be critical to managerial success. Through an annual process referred to as the Executive Development Review

(EDR), executive line management within each of the 40-plus operating units identifies the strengths, development needs, and corresponding promotability for approximately 100 managers within their respective operating units.

During 1987, a systematic research effort was conducted in which the EDR profiles of over 1,500 managers were carefully analyzed to determine those characteristics that best predicted promotability.[1] Following the analysis of more than 10,000 strengths and development needs associated with the 1,500 managers, seven core criteria were identified as the best predictors of executive potential.

1. *Intellectual Ability:* The ability to secure relevant information, relate and compare data from different sources, and identify issues and relationships; conceptual, analytical, creative.
2. *Results Orientation:* The ability to work toward outcomes and complete what one starts.
3. *Interpersonal Skills:* The ability to relate to the feelings and needs of others, and to convey interest and respect.
4. *Planning and Organizing:* The ability to schedule time and prioritize for self and/or others, to handle multiple activities, and to meet deadlines.
5. *Team Orientation:* The ability to work collaboratively within a complex organization structure.
6. *Maturity:* The willingness to be open and act responsibly when dealing with people and situations.
7. *Presence:* The ability to create a positive first impression and stand out tactfully (includes verbal and nonverbal communication).

These seven core criteria must be considered when selecting any employee for a position within the Baxter organization. Whether a person is being selected from the college campus into an entry level position, or is someone who is being considered for an internal promotion, these seven criteria must be examined as relevant evaluations. The core criteria are then supplemented by job-specific criteria that address the uniqueness of the position at hand.

The core criteria also move full circle to play a role in the Executive Development Review, providing consistency between selection standards and the annual assessment of the organization's talent base. In August 1988, Loucks and his Senior Management Committee devoted two days to an Executive Development Review of the top 100 executives at Baxter. Differences emerged in the development needs between high- and low-promotability managers.

Three observations may be made regarding low promotability. First, low promotability is characterized by a greater number of development needs. Second, the development needs associated with low promotability are more difficult to develop than the development needs more characteristic of high promotability. And third, the "core criteria" are more frequently identified as development needs for the low promotability category. For Baxter International, these observations begin to capture the selection standards for senior executives. When selecting an individual with senior management potential, this analysis suggests devoting serious consideration to avoid individuals who lack sufficient intellectual ability, maturity, and/or presence.

THREE TYPES OF TEAMS: SELECTION CONSIDERATIONS

In Chapter 3 on team structure, we identified three broad goals that seem to characterize why teams are assembled: (1) to solve problems; (2) to create something; or (3) to execute a well-defined task. Our research suggests that each of these three types of teams requires certain personal characteristics that are highly desirable for team members to possess. Table 4.1 refers to selection criteria for each of the three types of teams.

Problem-resolution teams must rely on trust in order to address issues effectively. According to the teams we interviewed, the people who seem to do best on problem-resolution teams possess some common characteristics. They are people who are intelligent: that is, conceptual enough to see relationships and analytical enough to reduce problems to meaningful issues. They are also, however, "street-smart" people who know how to read the pulse of a problem, not get caught up in "administrivia" and are able to concentrate on getting things done. They are sensitive to the interpersonal needs of other team members so as not to complicate issue analysis with relationship snags. And, perhaps most important to the establishment of and reliance on trust, effective problem-resolution team members must possess a high degree of integrity. They are fully aware that *trust begets trust.*

Creative team members, while very similar to those people who

TABLE 4.1
Selection Criteria

Broad Objective	Dominant Feature	Process Emphasis	Dominant Selection Criteria	Examples
1. Problem Resolution	Trust	Focus on issues	• Intelligent • "Street smart" • People sensitive • High integrity	• American Leadership Forum • Centers for Disease Control • *Challenger* investigation team • Presidential Cabinet • Executive management teams
2. Creative	Autonomy	Explore possibilities and alternatives	• Cerebral • Independent thinkers • Self-starters • Tenacious	• IBM PC team • McDonald's Chicken McNugget team • US Space Command • Boeing 747 team • Theatrical productions
3. Tactical	Clarity	Directive Highly focused tasks Role clarity Well-defined operational standards Accuracy	• Loyal • Committed • Action-oriented • Sense of urgency • Responsive	• Cardiac surgery teams • USS *Kitty Hawk* crew • Sports teams • Mountain-climbing teams

seem to do best on problem-resolution teams, possess personal characteristics that are somewhat unique. Creative teams also do best with members who are intelligent. Intelligence for the creative team member, however, takes a slightly different twist in that they are highly "cerebral." Not only are they conceptual and analytical, but they are also capable of abandoning normative thinking, exploring "possibilities" that extend beyond historical approaches to problems and traditionally accepted solutions. Put rather bluntly, the most effective people on creative teams possess a cognitive approach which, on a day-to-day basis, might appear a bit unusual. They are always talking about "possibilities," and "what if's." They are, in short, independent thinkers.

In addition, the more effective members on creative teams are self-starters who take a personal interest in the team's objective. It is not unusual for highly effective members on creative teams—the IBM PC team, McDonald's Chicken McNugget team, the Boeing 747 airplane project—to find themselves working on weekends and during the evening, and to be thinking about the problem all the time.

Finally, members of the creative teams possess a high degree of confidence and tenacity. Their ability to be creative is not easily discouraged by the persistence of the blank piece of paper day after day, or the raised eyebrows of others. Nor is their creative rhythm easily discouraged by the absence of immediate solutions.

Tactical teams, which focus on the operational execution of a task, also require team members who possess certain dominant personal characteristics. Our sample of team interviewees—people who were members of cardiac surgery teams, the USS *Kitty Hawk*, sports teams, or mountain-climbing teams—consistently reported the following qualities as being necessary to make such teams function like the proverbial "well-oiled machine." It is necessary for members of tactical teams to be highly responsive. When it is time to execute an assigned task that is part of the technical effort, such execution must occur almost automatically.

Typically, tactical teams are characterized by small margins of error. The name of the game for tactical teams is precision in terms of a consistent quality of response and dependability in terms of timing. Such demands require individuals who are highly action-oriented and possess a sense of urgency. This dominant feature of tactical team members should also be supplemented by people who enjoy and desire a strong team identification.

Part of the magic of highly successful tactical teams is the great sense of commitment people feel toward the team, its objective, other members, and the concept of team success. Usually, the results and success of a tactical team are easily measured. The open heart surgery is either successful, or it is not. The football team either wins or it loses. The aircraft carrier completes its mission, or it does not. The mountain-climbing team either reaches the peak, or it falls short. There is a transference of success in terms of team identification. If the team is successful, if the team is a winner, then the individual is successful and a winner. It is important for tactical teams to attract people who find the challenge of performing and winning to be appealing. That is the personal characteristic that most easily translates into loyalty and a commitment toward making the team successful.

The distinctions among team members that appear to suit best the three broad-brush types of teams are considerations worth making when selecting team members. Our research strongly suggests that properly matching the personal characteristics of a potential team member to the broad-brush objective can avoid frustration to the individual, other team members, and certainly the designated team leader. As cardiac surgeon Don Wukasch remarked:

> I think there is a preselection factor of people who tend to enjoy different types of responsibilities. Paying attention to this preselection can increase the chances of bringing people together on a team who share in a similar system of values. This greatly increases the chances of success.

THREE COMMON FEATURES OF
COMPETENT TEAM MEMBERS

On a more general level, three variables emerged from our research that appear common to the selection of team members for any successful team.

1. The essential skills and abilities. Not much can be accomplished if team members do not possess the skills, abilities, and knowledge that are relevant to the team's objective. Such abilities and skills are typically technical in nature, but the notion of technical skills in this sense covers a wide spectrum. The more obvious end of the spectrum involves what might be thought of as the hard technical skills. However, there are also technical skills that are not so well defined, as best exemplified by Dr. Lyle Conrad of the Centers for Disease Control. As Dr. Conrad pointed out, the primary technical skill for an effective epidemiologist, whose responsibility is investigative research, is "an individual prepared to think right."

2. *A strong desire to contribute.* When Boeing is awarded a large contract, one of the next key steps is "THE DRAFT"—the identification, selection, and assignment of those people who are best suited to work on the project. According to Joe Madden, in charge of the Small ICBM programs at Boeing, it's always important to talk to those people who might become part of the team in order to find out a little bit about their personal needs and desires, and how such needs might either support or be in conflict with the team's objective. Such was the case when selecting members to prepare Boeing's bid for the Small ICBM Weapon Control System. As Madden recalled:

> We had one guy come in and say, "I've got to paint my house this summer. I would really like to work on this project, but you've got to understand I've got to paint my house." So we said, "go paint your house and don't worry about this project. It's okay. We understand."

A bit more subtle, but equally important, is the frustration that arises when an individual team member does not make a connection between his contributions and the overall success of the team. This more subtle dimension of "contribution" is more apt to be found in teams where roles and responsibilities are of a more general nature, such as with executive management teams. Each of the CEOs we interviewed commented specifically that one of the hardest things to do on a management team is to get people to see how important it is for each member to contribute actively to the team. All in all, there is a dramatic difference in the performance of a team when team members work at finding ways of contributing.

3. *The capability of collaborating effectively.* A consistent response from the interviewees in our sample was the importance of selecting team members who were capable of working well with others. The emphasis in their responses was on capability. It was noted, repeatedly, that some people are capable of dealing with others in a collaborative fashion, and some are not. Some people are capable of focusing on issues instead of positions, capable of sharing information

openly, capable of listening objectively to fellow team members, and capable of bringing out the best in others. Some people are simply not "wired-up" that way.

In fact, one of the strongest and most persistent messages that emerged from our data was the necessity of removing people from teams who were not capable of collaborating effectively with others. The common message from our sample of interviewees was simple and direct: There is no longer any room on teams for people who cannot work collaboratively. Ruth Rothstein, CEO of Mt. Sinai Hospital in Chicago, summarized this sentiment best:

> One person who doesn't work well with others can set the team off into oblivion. One person like this can ruin a team. When that happens, you give feedback to that individual and help them make the necessary changes. But if they can't adapt, then you have an obligation to remove them from the team. Otherwise, the rest of the team can become pretty resentful.

CONFIDENCE IN THE TEAM

When strong technical skills are combined with a desire to contribute and an ability to be collaborative, the observable outcome is an elevated sense of confidence among team members. This confidence, in turn, translates into the ability of a team to be self-correcting in its capacity to adjust to unexpected adversity and emergent challenges. When people believe in each other, when they believe that each team member will bring superior skills to a task or responsibility, that disagreements or opposing views will be worked out reasonably, that each member's view will be treated seriously and with respect, that all team members will give their best effort at all times, and that everyone will have the team's overall best interest at heart, then excellence can become a sustainable reality.

If selecting team members who are talented, want to make a contribution, and work well with others seems like a difficult challenge, it's because it is. But, it's not impossible. Reflecting upon the interview process as the most common means for identifying success characteristics, the chairman and CEO of Emerson Electric, Charles F. Knight, put this difficulty into focus: "If you have a good interview you can get at all that stuff. There aren't a lot of good candidates out there. That's what makes it easy!"

NOTE

1. The analysis of the core criteria was conducted by Dr. Alan Resnick and Michele Yanta of Baxter Healthcare Corporation and Dr. Susan Stein of Omni Research and Training.

5

Unified Commitment

So far we've identified three broad factors that contribute to the effectiveness of a team: a clear, elevating goal; a results-driven structure; and competent team members. The important, but often elusive fourth factor—unified commitment—has a qualitatively different character to it. Thus, while unified commitment is often the most clearly missing feature of ineffective teams, it is difficult to know precisely what it is.

Certainly, it is "team spirit." It is a sense of loyalty and dedication to the team. It is an unrestrained sense of excitement and enthusiasm about the team. It is a willingness to do anything that has to be done to help the team succeed. It is an intense identification with a group of people. It is a loss of self. "Unified commitment" is very difficult to understand unless you've experienced it. And even if you have experienced it, it is difficult to put into words.

Jim Lynch, captain of the championship Notre Dame football team, had this to say about his team:

When I was captain of the team I took it so damn seriously it's unbelievable. To this day I still believe that's the greatest honor I ever had in playing. I made All-American, All-Pro, and won the Maxwell trophy, but those things never meant as much to me as being captain of that football team. I believed in it so much; I believed in the people who were there; and I believed in Notre Dame. . . . It was kind of a magical time. It was a time when everybody worked their hind end off. I can hardly explain it, but it really was a group of guys that believed in what they were doing. The coach instilled that. He took a team that was two and seven my freshman year, and the next year [1964] we went nine and one and almost won the national championship. . . . We had the players, we were coached so well, and we believed so much in what we were doing. You would have kids that would get hurt in the middle of a

game and would literally crawl off the field so they wouldn't have to
call time out. It wasn't like that was a big deal, that's just what you
naturally did. I never felt that again with any other team. Amazing
stuff.

Now don't make the mistake of assuming that these feelings happen only on college football teams. Joe Sutter spoke of a similar
enthusiasm among the Boeing 747 team members:

There's still some excitement in the commercial airplane business. That
first flight of the airplane has grandeur. It gives the guys a sense of
satisfaction. Seeing that airplane fly . . . it's hard to describe.

We saw a lot of highly successful, hard-driving people get misty-
eyed and melancholic about teams they had been on. That experience, being part of a team—especially a successful team—is unique.
And if that feeling can be understood and somehow fostered, collective efforts will surely improve.

To that end, we will discuss first two components of this feeling:
commitment—or dedication to the endeavor itself, and *unity*—or intense identification with the team. Second, we'll discuss ways of fostering unified commitment.

UNIFIED COMMITMENT: THE COMMITMENT PIECE

Dr. Don Wukasch, a member of both the Michael DeBakey and
Denton Cooley cardiac surgery teams, described his intense commitment to those teams:

Nothing was as important for me as being on that team and making it
through the 10 years to get there. It was a total commitment, and when
I got married, that was part of the deal with my marriage. We looked at
it and never had any questions as to what came first. It was the job,
making that team. I think people who do that sort of thing have long
ago given up any other values.

Commitment/dedication—this was the distinguishing feature of
the people we met in our study of effective teams. But what is commitment? Simply, it is mental and physical energy. You can have a clear

and elevating goal, a well-designed team, and competent team members, but the minimum requirement for team success is effort. This is what Anundsen (1979) concluded from her analysis of teamwork among managerial women. Teams do not excel without serious individual investment of time and energy.

In Chapter 4, we reviewed the characteristics considered important in selecting individuals with high potential for contributing to team success. High on that list was a willingness to commit time and effort, the willingness to work hard, to do whatever is necessary to accomplish the goal.

Admiral Tom Lynch believes that effort is the minimal requirement for success. In commanding a Navy destroyer or captaining the Annapolis football team, Admiral Lynch recalled the most noteworthy successes as coming when everyone was working together and working hard to make it happen. This is equally true on a ship and in football, as Lynch commented:

> You've got a Roger Staubach who is a Heisman award winner and Mr. All-everything to the third-string quarterback who knows he's not going to get in the big game on Saturday. Yet the third-string quarterback has to be motivated and think positive thoughts about the game on Saturday and the people he is working with if the whole team is going to be successful. If he is grumbling and complaining and taking up the coach's time and talking to everybody about what a bad deal he's getting, then that's going to affect everybody around him. So they either have to kick him off the team or get him thinking positively.

So much of team success involves intangibles, qualities like attitudes and energies. The teams we investigated that accomplished truly remarkable things—or that functioned unusually well in more routine activities—were always characterized by genuine dedication to the goal and a willingness to expend extraordinary amounts of energy to achieve it. Joe Jaworski, founder of the American Leadership Forum, has personally witnessed some exceptional teams and unusual team accomplishments. Jaworski said about team commitment:

> When you have people who come together and do something that is almost unbelievable, what makes that happen? What we think we've identified involves several things. One is a clear common purpose:

There isn't any question about what they have to do. The other is that
everybody buys into that goal and puts their personal self behind it. It's
not that they're doing it because they're getting paid for it, or whatever
motivations normally occur. It's that they've decided that it's *my personal worth* that's involved here, *me personally*. An increased sense of
self, but also a commitment of self into the project.

This combining of energies and balancing of identities leads to the
second component of unified commitment, the unity dimension.

UNIFIED COMMITMENT: THE UNITY DIMENSION

When the Raiders played the Dolphins for the American Football
Conference Championship in 1973, the Raiders were a heavily penalized team with a "nasty" reputation. When the Raiders came to town
they came not only to play football; they came to "kick ass." They
dressed in silver and black, and their mood matched their colors.
They liked to try to intimidate—some would say bully—opposing
teams. And even in a sport that thrives on an image of toughness, the
Raiders stood out. Complaints were lodged with the National Football League Commissioner about their rough style of play, and some
members of opposing teams threatened lawsuits and criminal
charges.

The Dolphins were one of the least penalized teams in the NFL.
They ran on skill and precision. They were smooth, polished profes-
sionals who executed flawlessly and frequently out-thought, as well as
out-played their opponents.

Who won the game is for our purposes irrelevant. The point is that
they were both effective and successful teams. And the point is not
which identity is better. The point is that both teams had an identity
that coalesced and unified the team. Both teams stood for something,
operated according to a common set of values, and were clear about
what kind of team each was. The important thing about team identity
is not that it's the right one, or the best one, or the most appropriate
one, but that whatever the identity is, it unifies.

In an analysis of management teams, Sherwin (1976) concluded
that group spirit and teamwork are indispensable to superior performance. But group spirit and teamwork come about as a result of
identification with a team. In that identification there is a relinquish-

ing of the self—not a denial of the self, but a voluntary redefinition of the self to include membership in the team as an important aspect of the self. There is a blurring of the boundaries between self and others—an increase in the emotional commerce, an open exchange between self and others.

Perhaps some sense of this identification process can be discerned in the following excerpt from our interview with Jim Seymour, another member of the championship Notre Dame football team:

> I went down in the Oklahoma game before half-time, tore an ankle apart. Oklahoma had a good team at the time. It was a vicious game. The guys came in at half-time and I was with the doctor. Every guy who came in said, "Jim, we're going to get 'em." By the time I came out of the locker room in the third quarter, on crutches and with a cast on, they had already put seven of the other guys out of the game. The rout was on. But I'll tell you what's really sad. We were getting ready to play Navy, and I wanted to go with the team so bad. Even though I couldn't play because I was still on crutches, I wanted to get on that airplane. Be with them. I was crushed that I couldn't go with my team.

This exceptionally intense emotional bonding and identification was reported by many of the teams in our sample. The sense of unity was present when members of the Petro-Lewis Corporation were putting together financial arrangements never before attempted in the oil industry. It was there in the Monday morning planning sessions of the IBM "Boca Raton" team, in the cardiac surgery teams, and the mountain-climbing teams. That sense of unity comes about as a result of commitment to a clear and worthwhile goal and the relinquishing of the self to the team that is in pursuit of that goal.

FOSTERING UNIFIED COMMITMENT

Unified commitment is a very amorphous property of successful teams. It is difficult even to conceptualize, let alone deliberately and systematically build. Having a clear and worthwhile goal helps considerably. But beyond the significance of the activity itself, there are several recurring themes identified by team leaders and members as having a positive effect on the emotional tone, spirit, or identification with the team.

Involvement enhances commitment. Contemporary knowledge
about teamwork supports the conclusion that there is a direct positive
relationship between involvement and commitment (Dyer, 1977). Participation, especially in the planning of strategies for achieving goals,
increases motivation, effort and, ultimately, success. The people we
talked to were absolute and unequivocal in endorsing the principle of
involving team members in the development of plans for achieving
the goal. The extraordinary success of Alvarado Construction was
explained by Linda Alvarado, in part, as "taking people out of their
normal responsibilities and giving them the opportunity to be involved in something entirely different."

The prototypical model of involvement, as described by team leaders we talked to, has two phases. First, the leader needs to become
crystal clear in terms of the goal and the consequences of achieving or
not achieving it. The leader must be able to articulate that goal in a
way that inspires commitment. If the members can be involved in
defining the goal or shaping the vision, all the better. More typically,
however, involvement occurs in the second phase when team members become actively engaged in planning strategies for achieving the
goal.

Although we found this two-phase conceptualization of involvement across the board, in all types of teams, the context in which it
was most interesting was the theater. Producer/director Paul Lazarus
explained it as follows:

> There is a distinction between the director as the leader and actors as
> the followers. But I think that when everyone has a clear goal—that I
> as the director offer the actors—once the goal has been established, the
> line of demarcation between the director as leader and actors as follow-
> ers completely breaks down—to the point where I lose complete sight
> of my usual role as director and we feed off each other.

If Paul Lazarus, of the theater, and Linda Alvarado, of the construction industry, were ever to meet, they might be amazed at how similar
their roles as team leaders are.

Commitment enhanced by involvement is a straightforward and
consistent theme. But the second issue associated with fostering unified commitment is a far more complex and perplexing one. This
issue involves a delicate balance between respecting individual differences and requiring unity. It involves the issue of how much of the self

is retained after relinquishing some individual identity to the team. In social science terms, it involves a balance between differentiation and integration (e.g., Eichhorn, 1974).

Balancing differentiation and integration. There is a delicate balance in teams between appreciating individual differences and requiring unity. The extremes, of course are easily identified. When the emphasis shifts too far toward requiring unity, what frequently results is conformity, "groupthink," and the stifling of creativity and divergent thinking. The typically cited extreme case is the failed Bay of Pigs invasion plan implemented by the Kennedy Cabinet, in which some individual Cabinet members failed to voice their concern with the plan. At the other extreme is the conflicted group, the team that suffers from analysis paralysis, the multiple-identity group that suffers so much from conflicts of vision and values that it is immobilized. We have all undoubtedly experienced just enough of both extremes to recognize how crucial it is to avoid those conditions. The problem is that having avoided the extremes, the merits of alternative choices become less clear cut. Take a very typical, mid-range set of circumstances:

You are the general manager of a company that specializes in a customized product that is used as a subsystem in a larger system manufactured by your end-user customers. You've been confronted by several angry customers, and after discussing the problems with your executive management team, your understanding of the situation is this:

Marketing contracted with one of your customers to deliver a customized subsystem, promising delivery within six weeks. It's unclear whether this promise was made because Marketing is a relatively new function in this newly formed organization; whether its members are just very competitive by nature; whether they really believed in the delivery date; or whether they thought the product was already fairly well-designed. In fact, it wasn't.

The design engineers scrambled to meet the deadline. The factory was told of the situation two weeks later and said, "Here we go again." Marketing checked with Manufacturing and said, "How are we doing?" and Manufacturing said, "We don't even have it from design." Four weeks into the project the program manager had to give the customer a progress report, and the customer panicked.

You haven't negotiated a new delivery date, so the customer is expecting to fulfill his plans on schedule. Marketing is pressuring manufacturing to deliver. Manufacturing has many more "top priorities" than it can handle. The team can't possibly meet the six-week deadline; in fact, they'll be lucky to be ready in 16 weeks. The situation has become highly personalized. Marketing is seen as a bunch of unprincipled hucksters who will promise anything. Manufacturing is seen as a bunch of unmotivated, feet draggers who specialize in making excuses. Design is seen as a bunch of spaced-out dreamers out of touch with reality and impossible to talk to.

Let's say that you respond to the team structure problem by doing what a lot of other organizations have done: You institute project teams that are composed of representatives from Marketing, Design, and Manufacturing. You reintegrate the goals at that next higher level, the new project teams. You have involved your own direct reports in developing a clear understanding of the problem, analyzing the issues, and developing the strategy for responding to the problem. But even after the structural changes are made—so that the project teams consisting of members from Marketing, Design, and Manufacturing now work directly and intensely with the customer in planning all stages of the project—things go from bad to worse. There is so much loyalty to, and identification with the individual functions of Marketing, Design, and Manufacturing, that now members of the project teams play out their hostilities, in subtle but very recognizable ways, in front of the customer.

As this case illustrates, one of the most serious threats to the success of a team is the conflict between individual and team goals. Moreover, if unified commitment is absent, establishing a new team structure does little to help. The following represents the most consistent advice from the respondents about how to handle this general problem.

Dr. Don Wukasch, talking about cardiac surgery teams, stressed that you have to be clear about your mission, and there has to be a commonality of purpose.

> If there is not a commonality of purpose, for whatever reasons, you can't build an effective team. Team members have got to believe that what they are doing is more important than anything else. If some people don't feel that way, don't try to change their minds. Let them go.

Duke Drake, discussing the management teams at Dun and Bradstreet, said:

If you are leading a team of smart guys, they will spot really quickly if someone is doing things for his own reasons, and they'll resent it. The biggest detriment to team effectiveness is ego. When someone says how can this make me look good, he's done.

George McLeod told this story about a self-serving team member on an expedition to Antarctica:

There are a lot of real hard rules, but as a team, you have to abide by them. The moment you find someone who is dodging their job, you take them in hand and explain to them that we need to work as a team.

There was a chap on the Antarctic expedition. It's really funny how cunning he was. When you got your bath day (which with a group of 17 was every 17 days), what you did was cut into the snow, melt it, and heat it up. Then you poured it into the tub, stripped off your clothes, climbed into the tub, and you had a bath. The minute you finished your bath you pulled in all your dirty clothes and stuck them into the hot water and walked on them.

Well, during most of my baths there would be a knock at the door, and this chap would say, "George, could you do this shirt for me; it's the cleanest one I have, and it's so filthy." I said, "Sure I'll wash it." Every night a different person would be having a bath and every night this fellow would get his sheets washed, his pants, shirts. Somebody said, "I did John's shirt the other day," and I said, "Wait a minute, I did John's shirt the other day also." Well it's amazing in tough circumstances how that undermines the team. Someone's getting away with something and no one likes it. If people are fair, then a team will function well.

For example, we had a kid who was so sick he was in bed for almost four months. We functioned fine. We took him to the bathroom and we bandaged his legs and feet every night. It wasn't just one person either and it wasn't by vote. It wasn't your turn tonight, my turn tomorrow. It was a case of people just coming in and saying "Kenny, what can I do for you?" A team is a group of people pulling together. It's not the actual work, it's the principle of fairness.

Joe Madden manager of many successful projects, including one of the largest and most complex projects underway in this country, the basing elements for the Small ICBM (Midgetman), said:

There were circumstances in which a team member wasn't contributing or wasn't fitting in. I could see what the problem was and I had to sometimes fight off the ones on the team who wanted to get that person out. I would talk to that person, get my expectations clear, make sure we understood each other. I would talk to the team about their expectations of other people, how much that person was doing, and how much real appreciation they had for what he was doing. But if nothing changed, that guy is gone. He can't stay on any longer.

One perspective on the problem we found particularly insightful came from Baxter International's Anthony Rucci, who has observed these issues being played out in one of their most intense contexts—corporate mergers. Rucci reminded us that all people have their own agenda in life, things they are trying to accomplish that they want to feel good about. So a certain level of individual differentiation must be tolerated. And in fact, there are many situations in which high levels of individual achievement and success are not only accepted, but are celebrated by the team—as long as that individual achievement comes as a result of working toward the team goal.

If the individual is expending effort toward the team goal, then all kinds of differentiation can be both accepted and appreciated. But if the individual's effort is going toward purely personal goals, then the team will recognize this and ostracize the person. According to Rucci:

It's a difficult thing to put your finger on because the two behaviors—one self-serving and one striving for results—look very similar. At a behavioral level you wouldn't see a whole lot of difference. So as a team leader, you have to be careful. But there are subtle things you see happening in those two different situations. The person who is doing things that are self-serving is probably not going to pick up another member of the team when they stub their toe. It's going to be more a reaction of taking advantage of it or putting their head down and going even harder. So there are subtle cues that you pick up on. But it is dysfunctional to a team. And when I think about it, my honest reaction is you can't tolerate individuals pursuing their own agenda, you have to eliminate them from the team.

So the second factor that's related to unified commitment, the unity dimension, can be fostered by recognizing that team members have high expectations for each other, expect that everyone on the team will contribute to the extent that each is capable, and will become disturbed if a member pursues individual objectives *at the expense of the team goal*. When the situation is present, the best advice seems to be to discuss the situation individually with the person who seems self-serving or noncontributing; to develop a clear understanding of expectations for that individual, in as concrete or behavioral terms as possible; to give the individual a fair opportunity to demonstrate change; and then, if nothing happens, to remove the individual from the team.

In most of the effective teams we examined, there is a delicate balance between differentiation and integration. Occasionally, we have been genuinely surprised with the results of our investigation. This is an area in which we find ourselves most surprised. If you believe that we have emphasized integration at the expense of appreciating individual member differences, you can share with us another surprise when we get to Chapter 10. If you examine the 32 intact management teams we've studied since completing the descriptive part of this research, and you ask what is both the most consistent and most intense complaint that team members have about team leaders, it is not that leaders fail to recognize and/or appreciate the individual contributions to team success or the individual merits of team members. Rather, the complaint is that team leaders are unwilling to confront and resolve problems involving individual performance. More than any other single aspect of team leadership, members are disturbed by leaders who are unwilling to deal directly and effectively with self-serving or noncontributing team members.

6

Collaborative Climate

The essence of teams is teamwork. If a team is a group of people pursuing a specific performance objective, the achievement of which requires coordinated action, then teamwork must be a significant factor in determining a team's success. Teamwork is the cumulative result of all the factors we've talked about so far: Teamwork is, above all else, influenced by the clarity and the significance of the goal. Teamwork takes place within a structure that either facilitates or impedes effective coordination of effort. Teamwork is more likely to succeed if members are both competent in the technical knowledge and skills associated with the performance objective and able to collaborate effectively with one other. And teamwork succeeds most dramatically when team members are enthusiastically unified in pursuit of a common objective rather than individual agendas.

In accounting for the success of collective efforts, however, teamwork even goes beyond these factors—existing as a factor in its own right. Often, when the team exceeds what could be reasonably predicted from a knowledge of the member's abilities, such unusual outcomes are frequently explained in terms of some internal dynamic operating either within the team or between the team members and the leader.

Triumphs of teamwork occur everywhere but are most frequently documented in sports, where performance objectives and outcomes are very clear cut and where extensive monitoring of both team and individual performance levels is commonplace. It is in the sports arena where the adage "the whole is greater than the sum of the parts" can be most easily demonstrated. Stanley Cohen (1982) offers the following impressive examples:

> The most imposing winning skein in sports is owned by the Boston Celtics. From 1957 to 1969, the Celtics won the NBA Championship

eleven times, without once having a player among the top three scorers in the league. It was much the same with the 1949–53 Yankees, who won five World Series with players who never led the league in any major batting department. Their lineup never was as strong as Boston's or Cleveland's, never had the punch of the Dodger teams they beat three times in that span. (p. 20)

"Working well together" is such a fundamental ingredient in team success that it was mentioned by our interviewees as a significant characteristic of the effectively functioning teams they had experienced. From the incredibly specific and intricately coordinated safety-related activities of mountaineering teams; to the sharing of information, opinions, visions, judgments, and data of highly creative project teams; to the total interdependence, individual accountability, and interlocking responsibilities of military teams, "working well together" was recognized by everyone as something important.

In our interviews, "working well together" was typically characterized in one of two ways. First, it was sometimes attributed to structural features of teams, such as clearly differentiated roles, responsibilities, and accountabilities, or clear lines of communication, record keeping, and documentation. Second, it was often characterized as a feeling or climate that described relationships among members of the team or between the team and its leader. It was usually a climate that fostered collaboration, and interviewees, when pushed, almost always explained this climate by referring, in one way or another, to "trust."

Trust is one of those mainstay virtues in the commerce of mankind. It is the bond that allows any kind of significant relationship to exist between people. Once broken, it is not easily—if ever—recovered.

Our content analysis of the data indicates that trust is produced in a climate that includes four elements: (1) honesty—integrity, no lies, no exaggerations; (2) openness—a willingness to share, and a receptivity to information, perceptions, ideas; (3) consistency—predictable behavior and responses; and (4) respect—treating people with dignity and fairness.

The problem, according to our sample of interviewees, is that trust is so fragile that if any one of the elements listed above is breached— even once—a relationship is apt to be severely compromised, even lost. In fact, our research shows a predictable pattern of diminishing confidence once a trusting relationship is violated (see Figure 6.1).

For example: If someone with whom you have a relationship (at

86

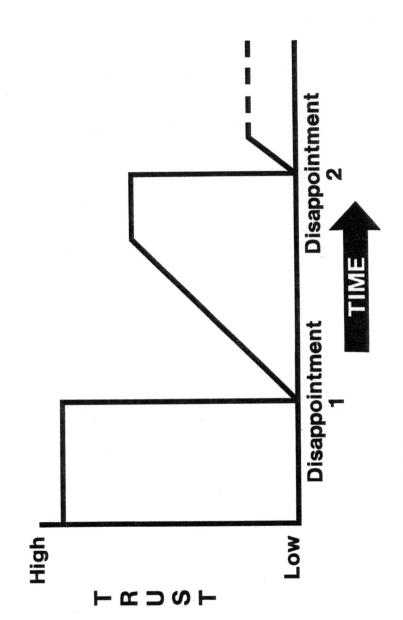

Figure 6.1: When Trust Is Broken

work or socially) lies to you, your trust in that person collapses to zero. Instantly. It is, in effect, a catastrophic event. What's more, a suspicion is born—prompting you to review and reevaluate events from the past—that perhaps the relationship had never been honest. People may try to rebuild a relationship after the initial breach, but they can rarely restore it to its original luster. And if the same person lies to you a second time, the relationship stands little chance of surviving. At best, it becomes clouded by hesitancy and doubts, becoming barely functional.

With trust gone between individuals, teams have little hope of functioning well and realizing their true potential.

Our research further emphasizes the significance of trust by eludicating what it allows teams to be, to do, and to accomplish.

COLLABORATION FLOURISHES IN A CLIMATE OF TRUST

Anthony Rucci was one of the team leaders who expressed a special appreciation for the value of trust:

> If there is one thing in my mind that characterizes the really effective teams I've been involved with, it's trust. It's trust at a couple of levels. You need to clearly define the expectations, leaving people with the sense that you trust them enough to do things on their own, that you trust their judgment enough to let them take some personal initiative, that you are not looking over their shoulder. That is the quickest way that I know of for the manager of a team to demonstrate trust and to build a climate for trust. Beyond that, I think trust comes in most clearly in honesty, a sense of integrity in the way people deal with one another within the team.

Joe Jaworski, founder and chairman of the American Leadership Forum, has reached a similar conclusion. When asked to identify key characteristics of the effectively functioning teams he has experienced, Jaworski replied:

> I think one of the key things is trust. Trust and communication is really the same thing for me. I'm talking about where you really trust a person to lay it all out—the kind of trust where you may be willing to sit down and talk to a person about your deepest feelings. This kind of

trust does not normally exist. It builds as a result of things that people experience with each other. Good communication grows out of that kind of trust. and good communication is what you will always notice in effective teams.

In our examination of effectively communicating teams. four themes emerged to help explain why a climate of trust fosters teamwork.

1. Trust allows team members to stay problem-focused. The absence of trust diverts the mental concentration and energy of a team away from its performance objective and onto other issues. The team becomes politicized. Communication becomes guarded and distorted. Alliances and personal agenda begin to take precedence over the team goal. The resulting loss of focus on the common goal is a critical factor. It wounds the team and often renders it ineffective.

Conversely, when trust is present, a collaborative climate is more readily fostered—allowing team members to stay focused on their common problem or goal. There is no suspicion or conflict to divert their attention. The clearer the goal. and the more team members are free to concentrate on it. the greater the likelihood they will succeed.

Dr. Michael Gregg. speaking of teams associated with the Centers for Disease Control. spoke of trust as the first and most visible feature of effectively functioning teams:

> Probably the most important element is mutual trust. where you feel that there are no other ulterior motives in your team effort than to solve the problem. . . . You are all in the same room. You may have been doing different things for the last two or three days in an overall effort. but when you come together. there before you is the problem. If your attention goes all in the same direction. it develops a unity that is very important. Trust provides a climate conducive to the exchange of ideas. Without mutual trust. you may be embarrassed to bring up something you think is trivial. although it is something people should know. You may be unwilling to admit you're having a problem with something. You may be reluctant to say to someone "Watch out for so and so because I'm afraid you are not going to get good information from him."

Clearly. team problem-solving relies on the unhampered exchange of information and communication that is born of trust.

From an epidemiology team to a product-development team in the fast food industry, the impact of trust is the same. Bud Sweeney, leader of the Chicken McNugget team for McDonald's Corporation, expressed it in his own way:

> The people that I selected had an agreement. Our agreement was the best vote out of three. That was our rule. If two of us agreed on something, that's the way it flew. Win, lose, or draw. It wasn't personality, it was the complete devotion to the success of the project. I knew their purpose was singular and comparable to mine. I had no problem with it. I lost some, but I was very comfortable in saying, "My God, I don't want to lose this project." Three heads are better than one.

2. Trust promotes more efficient communication and coordination. Trust not only allows people to stay problem-focused, it promotes a more efficient use of the time and energy devoted to the problem. Captain Joe Prueher of the U.S. Navy Strike Warfare Center talked about the value of candor and honesty on the part of team members:

> You have to have a frank, candid exchange of communication. Often you've got to get something difficult done in a short period of time. You don't want to spend time trying to figure out what someone is really saying or how he is gaming this process. You need to have mutual confidence so people can communicate well.

In his review of climate factors that influence the effectiveness of organizational teams, Sullivan (1988) identified communicating candidly, confronting issues, and using each other's resourcefulness as factors that affect climate and increase the likelihood of teams attaining missions, goals, and objectives.

These are the same factors, incidentally, that have been observed to impact a team's ability to improve its own performance (Gavin & McPhail, 1978). Our own experiences in phase two of this research support the conclusion that trust is associated with efficiency of communication and coordination, especially in activities directed toward improving the team's understanding of its own performance. When our measurement and monitoring of an intact team discloses that trust is a problem for that team, we have learned that certain consequences are extremely likely. When we sit down with that team to discuss its profile and seek ways of improving its performance, the communication is likely to be guarded, very ambiguous, and difficult to understand. There appears to be a lot of maneuvering and a considerable amount of denial and defensiveness. Consequently, there is a constant need to refocus the issue at hand. This is a far less efficient process than typically emerges when the measurement indicates a high level of trust. Thus, trust not only characterizes a team that functions effectively in pursuit of its goal, it also characterizes a team that is self-correcting, better at examining and improving its own processes.

   3. Trust improves the quality of collaborative outcomes. This theme contains an important key to understanding what a collaborative climate is and what it accomplishes. The key involves understanding how two very subtle and potentially antagonistic norms can be maintained simultaneously in an effectively functioning team.

   The first norm involves being highly disclosive and sharing information openly, especially when that information is "negative." Consider the following statement from Joe Madden, one of the most experienced project team leaders we know:

> You have to have good communication. Without communication nothing functions. I would spend a lot of time, when work was done at the end of the day, chatting with people. When you do that you get feedback: "This guy is driving me nuts." "Well, why, what's wrong?" Without that kind of input you can't even be aware of problems. In every program or project that I work on, I always make it clear to the team that everybody runs into problems, and that people make mistakes. That's human. But what you have to do if you think you've got a problem is to tell somebody about it so we can all get together and help you solve it. The only way you're going to screw up is if you try to hide a problem that you've got, so that by the time we find out about it there's no way to straighten it out. You have to create an atmosphere in which people are willing to bring problems to you and feel secure in doing that.

In a similar vein, Joe Sutter, leader of the Boeing 747 team, stated, "The worst failing is a team leader who's a nonlistener. A guy who doesn't listen to his people—and that doesn't mean listening to them and then doing whatever the hell he wants to do—can make a lot of big mistakes."

The first team norm that's supported by trust is that members of the team must be willing to share information with each other, especially when that information is negative. If a team member is having problems figuring something out or making a decision, this is the kind of information that must be shared. Hiding negative information and not being willing to listen to negative information are norms that can be ruinous to team outcomes.

The second norm that must be promoted is for team members to take risks and be permitted to fail. Charles F. Knight, CEO of Emerson Electric, talks about a climate within which people are likely to make good decisions:

> The person who is trying to create this environment must permit people to fail. You must find a way to permit failure because without that you're not going to get innovation or change. You are not going to get a rethinking process that is so vital. You are going to have to let some people try some things that you are not too certain about. Hopefully, this is controlled because when it is uncontrolled, you get yourself in deep trouble. But the challenge is to let people reach out, let people make mistakes in a controlled fashion and get the job done.

It is relatively easy to make a mistake about what a good "team player" looks like. For example, some people might question whether an individual is a "team player" if he persists in laying out negative information; talking about a problem he needs help with; warning the team about a violation of its own standards; or pushing for clarity on an issue that most members of the team seem to understand. Yet, the facts might reveal that this person is committing his mental and emotional energy to the success of the team effort. On the other hand, Anthony Rucci views lack of participation as not honoring the responsiblities of a team player:

> You talk about trust in a group—one of the quickest ways to establish trust, beyond giving people autonomy, is for members of the group to be willing to take a risk. When you have members of a group who are very afraid to take a risk, very afraid to state their opinions openly in a group situation and run the risk of someone disagreeing with them, you never know what they are thinking. Even though you have ostensibly reached an agreement among the group as to what happened, you can never count on it because whether they agreed or disagreed, they

would never say so anyway. You can't count on the fact that they walked away sharing the vision that other people walked out of the room with. That issue of taking a risk, and I mean taking a risk at an emotional level with people on the team, is a real important act.

Trust improves the quality of collaborative efforts because with it, decisions are more in tune with what is in fact happening. Problems are raised and dealt with instead of hidden until they become disastrous. People are willing to try something because there's a chance that it might work rather than remain inactive because of their fear of failure. And if something internal to the team itself is interfering with the team's success, then that problem is more likely to be confronted and resolved.

4. Trust leads to compensating. One explanation that has been offered for why teams sometimes succeed—even beyond reasonable expectations for success—is that "compensating" arises. Compensating happens when one team member picks up the slack that occurs when another member falters. If a lot of compensating occurs, then a whole team is capable of pulling itself, collectively, to new levels of performance.

Compensating builds confidence. We have already referred to social science research that demonstrates a strong association between what you think you are capable of and your actual performance level. When a team is clear about its goal and unified in its effort, and at the same time no one fears being left behind, being criticized for failing, or being left on one's own without support, then that team is capable of reaching new heights and arriving at the goal as an intact unit.

If you've ever been a member of an underdog team that triumphed over "superior" opposition, if you've ever been a member of a team that overcame great obstacles only because you were convinced that together you could, you have experienced a rare form of exhilaration. In the realm of collaborative efforts, those triumphs occur much more frequently when team members are compensating for each other.

Summarizing research on teams that took place in England and Australia, Belbin (1981) wrote about the value of compensating:

> To summarize about winning teams, their main feature was their strength in those personal qualities and abilities associated with the key team-roles, together with a diversity of talent and personality making up the rest of the team. There was always someone suitable for any job

that came up. Even teams with something less than the ideal distribution of talents could compensate for shortcomings by recognizing a
latent weakness and deciding to do something about it. (p. 99)

BUILDING TRUST AND COLLABORATION

Having identified why trust and the building of a collaborative
climate is so important, the question remains: How do you build a
climate of trust and collaboration in a team? There are undoubtedly
many factors to consider and many approaches to promoting trust
and collaboration. The fundamental answer, however, is that team
trust and collaboration come about as a result of *involvement* and
autonomy.

Bud Sweeney, one of the most successful project leaders in our
sample, gave us an interesting insight into how collaboration is developed on his projects. First, he makes sure that the goal is crystal clear
and that everyone on the team is absolutely committed to the achievement of that goal. The team must be, he says, ready to walk through
brick walls in order to succeed. Then team members sit down together and wrestle with the question, "Now how in the hell are we
going to do it?" Trust and collaboration come from being involved in
planning the attack, working out the strategy for accomplishing the
goal, and knowing what the team's approach is going to be and how it
all fits together—recognizing that achieving the goal is going to de-
pend on how well the team works together in developing and implementing its strategy.

The dramatic success story of Alvarado Construction is due in no
small measure to heightened involvement of individuals from the top
all the way down through the organization in planning and implementing projects. If everyone knows the plan, then ambiguity is decreased. Team members don't have to tell themselves and each other
stories about what is happening and why certain things are being
done.

This clarity about purpose and plan feeds into the enthusiasm with
which a team pursues the objective. Lon McCain, CFO of Petro-
Lewis Corporation, emphasized this theme:

One of the great things about a team is that if people get their juices
flowing a little bit they come up with ideas that can lead someone

else to come up with an idea, and sometimes you can have a dramatic impact on the overall project. But it certainly has a lot to do with the pace and the enjoyment of doing it and the success of it. People kept in the dark is the most damaging thing. People being told what to do rather than making them feel like they're deciding for themselves what their role is going to be is what kills their enthusiasm.

Getting people involved and giving them autonomy is what promotes collaboration. Anthony Rucci underlined this point:

Allowing people a lot of autonomy once it is clear what has to be done, not feeling like you need to be involved in every discussion that might occur between members of the team, and just respecting people's rights as individuals independently of their being a member of the team, that's a subtle aspect of having a really effective team of individuals.

Involvement and autonomy are not the only factors that are important in building and maintaining a collaborative climate, but they were clearly identified by the interviewees as a good place to start.

There are many factors that influence a team's success and the way people feel about being members of that team. Collaborative climate is a very special aspect of that success. Collaborative climate refers to the extent to which members communicate openly, disclose problems, share information, help each other overcome obstacles, and discover ways of succeeding. Collaborative climate is the essence of teams; it *is* the "teamwork." It is thought of by team leaders and members more in terms of "trust" than in terms of any other concept. As Vernon Loucks, chairman and CEO of Baxter International, said, "Trust is something that is a must. Trust is so fundamental in terms of what a team has to value. It's never absent very long on any team. It can't be."

7

Standards of Excellence

In 1954 the four-minute mile was broken by England's Roger Bannister, marking the first time in recorded history that anyone had been observed to run the distance of one mile in under four minutes. Interestingly, shortly after Roger Bannister broke the four-minute mile, John Landy from Australia broke Bannister's time, setting a world record. Then, in the classic one-mile Bannister/Landy duel, held in the same year as part of the British Commonwealth Games in Vancouver, British Columbia, both men broke the four-minute mile once again, while racing against each other. Of greatest interest in this tale of extraordinary accomplishments is that following the Bannister/Landy race, the four-minute mile was broken several more times by several other runners during the following year. It is safe to assume that this unusual accomplishment was not due to a sudden increase in the physical abilities of each runner to follow Roger Bannister. Hardly. Rather, it is far more likely that it was due to a demonstrated raising of the standard of excellence.

PRESSURE TO PERFORM

At the broadest conceptual level, a standard consists of pressure to achieve a required or expected level of performance. Openly articulated or haphazardly implied, standards define those relevant and very intricate expectations that eventually determine the level of performance a team deems acceptable. Standards provide answers to such questions as: How much technical knowledge, skill, and ability is required? How much initiative and effort are team members expected to demonstrate? How are people expected to treat one another? How serious are deadlines? How are results to be achieved? And, ultimately, standards address the two questions that every team must ask: What are the rewards for success? What are the consequences for failure?

No matter how pressure to perform is exerted, such pressure eventually focuses on individual effort. Andre de la Porte (1974) and Sugarman (1968) arrived independently at the same conclusion: Qualitative individual excellence characterizes successful organized teams. It is individual effort that determines if a standard is missed, met, or exceeded. And, it is the exerted pressure to perform that creates a tailwind behind individual effort.

Pressure to perform may be exerted in several different ways and can come from a number of different sources.

1. *Individual standards* consist of those performance expectations that each member of the team embraces as personal pressure to achieve. Individual standards are derived from one's life experiences. They grow out of where we have been, what we have done, our successes, our failures, our aptitudes, our interests, the role models we have had, and the manner in which we've been reinforced to try harder and achieve more.

As might be assumed, it is easiest to create high team standards if high personal standards exist among team members. In fact, the pressure exerted by the performance of one individual, such as a Roger Bannister, can often stimulate others to perform better than they normally do. It is not unusual for the addition of a team member with high performance standards, be it a quarterback or a manager, to influence team performance positively.

Sometimes we simply need a picture of what excellence might look like. In such instances, one individual can influence, usually by example, other members to perform at a higher level. That is not to say, however, that excellence is not achievable with less than "all stars." In fact, the concept of all-star teams, which do not always deliver peak performance, is the best testimony to the fact that excellent teams are more than a collection of people, even if the people in question are excellent performers individually.

2. *Team pressure*, similar to that exerted by individuals, can eventually influence individual performance. The extent to which a team requires itself to meet its objectives and honors ways of working together to achieve those objectives determines the team standard. For example, it might be acceptable to deliver minimum levels of performance through questionable means, while treating each other shabbily. Or, it might be *unacceptable* to do anything less than

overachieve through the highest forms of individual integrity, while treating fellow team members with the highest level of personal and professional respect. As such, team pressure to meet high standards—those that require more of individuals than they would probably require of themselves—can enhance individual performance.

Conversely, team pressure to meet low standards can eventually erode individual performance. In other words, poor performance is not always due to the absence of pressure to perform. Sometimes it is due to the presence of pressure *not* to perform. While it may be disappointing to contemplate, there are team standards that can influence individuals to withhold accomplishments. Perhaps the most striking examples emerge from those work environments where pay rates are established according to amount or "pieces" of work completed. It is not unusual in such cases for work groups to pressure an individual into a slower pace and less output so as not to reduce the rate of pay, or simply so as not to make other team members look bad.

Whatever the outcome, there is a performance pressure that exists within the group or collective effort. Such team pressure may be present in varying degrees and can focus on positive or negative outcomes. However directed, team pressure creates team standards, which influence a level of performance that is eventually translated into a level of success.

3. The *consequences* of success or failure can exert pressure to create standards that make success most predictable. Perhaps the more dramatic consequences are those that are most immediate, such as those that can occur when climbing a mountain or performing open heart surgery. In either case, the consequences of poor standards can be swift and quite dramatic.

While not every team has to respond to the level of pressure exerted by being on the side of a mountain or in a surgical suite, there is some level of pressure connected with the consequences of every team effort. At a bare minimum, the consequence of failure is the act of failing itself. Individuals and teams alike perform according to some expected level of achievement that attempts to make the experience a satisfying and gratifying one. Rarely do individuals or teams set out to do something that makes them feel bad about themselves when the experience is over.

As Jim Lynch, the star middle linebacker for Notre Dame and later for the Kansas City Chiefs, remarked: "It's not just that winning is so important. It's that losing feels so shitty." Rarely do you see people boast about their association with something unsuccessful. It just isn't the way we're wired up! We avoid feelings of failure and seek out opportunities to feel successful.

Even mediocrity carries consequences. Unlike failure, which usually results in the discontinuation of an effort, the hallmark of mediocrity is persistence. It goes on and on. By definition, it is better than failure and less than success. As such, the consequence is the association with something that cannot be truly successful, but continues nonetheless. To quote famed radio announcer Paul Harvey, mediocrity is "the best of the lousiest and the lousiest of the best."

Even in cases where a team discovers that, for whatever reason, its objective is meaningless and should be abandoned, there is a tendency for some team members to cling to the effort as still being worthwhile. After all, to give up an effort once it is started is to admit that the effort was a failure of judgment from the outset. In short, our accomplishments are not only important as achievements, they also exert a demonstrable influence on our self-esteem.

Whether the consequences of a team's effort are life-threatening or merely ego-bruising, there is pressure associated with success or failure. Such pressure can influence the establishment of standards designed to reduce the risk of failure and increase the likelihood of success.

4. *External pressure* consists of any impelling or constraining forces outside the actual team that exert influence on the team's performance. Pressure from the larger organization in which a team exists is an example of such external pressure. Consider for a moment what occurs when an organization makes a large investment in a new product and creates a team to bring that product to market. It would be rare to see an organization assign such a task without placing expectations, or even demands on the team's performance.

As a case in point, when Boeing Corporation established a project team to create the most advanced airplane in the world, the Boeing 747, the organization took a very active interest in making the project successful. Boeing placed a five-year time frame on the project, exerted pressure to meet several types of requirements, and instituted processes for selecting the best people and methods for monitoring progress.

At an organizational level, if the project had failed it would have meant an inability not only to remain competitive but also to continue to employ thousands of people. Aware of such risks, the 747 team felt pressured to meet the needs of the customer it served—in this case, the larger organization of which the 747 team was a part.

External pressure can also be exerted by independent constituencies, such as the media. Consider, for example, the conditions that existed when President Reagan appointed the Rogers Commission to investigate the space shuttle *Challenger* disaster. The disaster was an enormous threat to the space program, a fact which paled by comparison to the tragic loss of seven lives. The American people and people around the world demanded to know what happened. The Commission hearings were broadcast live, preempting the regularly scheduled daytime television programs. Camera crews camped out on the sidewalks to record a glimpse of the commissioners and solicit an answer to a shouted question. As you might expect, pressure to communicate with the media was enormous. According to Lieutenant Colonel Thomas Reinhardt, executive secretary of the Presidential Commission, it was important not to allow incomplete data and early observations to create inaccurate conclusions. This meant tightly managing the outside pressure created by the media. As Reinhardt explained:

> We had the best people to serve as commissioners and run the investigation: former Secretary of State; first man on the moon; first American woman in space; father of the Boeing 747; a Nobel Laureate in physics; etc. So, it made sense to have the staff assume a low profile. During the life of the Commission, we never granted a single interview, nor let a single news camera delve into the operations of the staff.

5. The *team leader* represents the final source of pressure to perform. We've found that this kind of pressure is exerted through a leader's ability to capture the consequences of a team's effort in an inspiring, demanding, and achievement-oriented way. It's the chief of surgery who demands not only strict adherence to procedures, but also requires that improvements to the procedures be constantly explored. It's the leader of the mountain-climbing team who demands that safety standards not be violated under any circumstance. It's the CEO who is able to capture why it is important to achieve a business plan, not only in terms of financial implications, but also in terms of social obligations.

While leadership is explored more fully in Chapter 9, suffice it to say here that pressure comes from leaders who demand that a standard be upheld and then search for ways to cause improvements to occur. It's the leader who is never quite satisfied with a good team performance, let alone the status quo. It is the leader who attempts to make current practices obsolete before the competition—or worse yet, failure—does so first. It's the leader who constantly pushes the team to overcome inertia—through constant follow-up, by never accepting excuses for a lack of results, and by creating consequences for failure and rewards for excellence. It became readily apparent throughout the interviews we conducted that the achievement-oriented leader who focuses on such principles of excellence exerts a source of pressure that raises team standards.

STANDARDS MAKE A DIFFERENCE

Eventually, a standard is defined by individual performance. It's how each team member handles the execution of responsibility that determines performance. This message was consistent across our entire sample of interviewees, and was perhaps best exemplified by Anthony Rucci, one of the team leaders during the Baxter Travenol/ American Hospital Supply merger. Rucci's primary role during the merger was to establish and implement a selection process for determining how people at all levels in both companies would be selected for positions in the new organization. Rucci told how one employee raised the standard of excellence within this process:

> We had a lot of people involved in the candidate slating process. We even had people who were doing clerical tasks. So you say, how does excellence get instilled at that level? One of my favorite lines is that people with high standards are those people who do ordinary things in an extraordinary way. One of the more classic examples had to do with the way we filed things, kept track of documentation, and monitored the flow of critical information. I said to one of our planning specialists that once job offers were made, we wanted to make sure we had signed offer letters of acceptance for positions returned by a particular date, and they needed to be filed, and here's how I would like to have the files set up. She came back to me later saying, "I know what you told me you wanted me to do yesterday, but I really think that if we did it 'this' way, it would be a much more effective process, and we could keep track of things much better." It was a simple matter, but to me that was a standard of excellence. It was more than I had suggested or

required of her at a time when it would have been easy for her to be preoccupied with her own personal job concerns.

In a slightly different context, Charles Bowsher, Comptroller General of the United States, made the following comment regarding quality requirements that must be observed by his staff:

When we write a report, we often have to then testify before Congress about it. Sometimes we also have to discuss it in a television or radio interview. There is a whole world out there scrutinizing our work— Republicans and Democrats, liberals and conservatives, people who like your work and people who don't. That's the challenge. So we have a review process that every report goes through before it gets issued and everyone in GAO knows from the start that they have to do quality work in order to get through that process. Building successful teams to write excellent reports and conduct those quality reviews is essential to us. I tell my organization of my terrible dream—that we issue a report, and it explodes because the facts aren't right. We have high quality standards and a stiff quality review process because that's what our work requires. One big blow up and our hard earned credibility would very quickly evaporate. We can put out 800 other reports that are solid products, but if we have one that is wrong, it would do enormous damage to our reputation overnight. Consistently high quality work is the key to our survival.

Similarly, the importance of high standards was articulated by Joe Sutter, who as chief engineer of the Boeing project was responsible for designing the airplane, meeting customer requirements, and making sure the airplane would be certified. The standards for the project were established by a Design Objectives Criteria Book. Sutter talked about the importance of this document:

Whenever Boeing designs a new airplane, the first thing that is done is a Design Objectives Criteria Book is written on the criteria for that airplane. There is one statement, for instance, that the airplane will meet all FAA regulations. That's just one statement, but it covers a hell of a lot. It also says that we will meet all of the Boeing design conditions, too. Now the Design Objectives Criteria Book is a fairly thick book. It is never violated, in effect, without taking it right up through the top management of the company. That book is sacred, but it's a living, working document.

Sutter further commented on the significance of the DOC book by recalling its application in resolving a major design challenge:

> There was a time when we were having trouble with the weight of the airplane. You know, you put everything into it that everybody wants, and then you start getting too heavy. It's at a time like that when you're faced with making compromises. That period of time, which lasted for about a year, was a time when the team worked particularly well together to get the weight out and still not violate any of the basic design criteria that we had established for the airplane. No matter how Boeing is organized, they will always have that check and balance system in design work and certification and safety matters.

Whether the outcome is a corporate merger, a congressional briefing, or the grandeur of the first flight of a new airplane, the establishment of and adherence to high performance standards have a direct influence on the quality and value of the final product.

STANDARDS ARE HARD WORK

Standards are not achieved simply by setting them. Meeting standards is hard work. Director Paul Lazarus emphasized this point when he commented on how interesting it was to watch the effort singer/actress Angela Lansbury invested in rehearsals when he directed "A Stephen Sondheim Evening":

> Angela Lansbury did one song, and yet she requested more rehearsal time than anybody else simply because she would not go out on the stage unless she was prepared within an inch of her life. I really respect that kind of professionalism. When Angela Lansbury walks out on a stage, she is so confident of doing it perfectly that there is no possibility of it not being perfect. She rehearsed "Send in the Clowns," which is a relatively simple song, once a week for 10 weeks. We could have done it in one rehearsal, but that's the kind of perfectionism that someone like that strives for, and that's why Angela Lansbury is a major star.

It became apparent to us from the interviewees in our sample that standards are not an intellectual enterprise. In fact, standards have to be de-intellectualized. Standards must come out of the abstract in order to become meaningful. The more concrete the standard, the better. Once a standard is concrete, then performance against that standard can be measured. Consider, for example, the manner in which standards are established by mountain climbers.

Pat Dillingham, a member of the Mt. Kongur, China, expedition, began her climbing in the Pacific Northwest, where the terrain is mostly glaciers, mixed ice and rock conditions, and also volcanoes. When Dillingham moved to Colorado, the emphasis shifted to technical rock climbing. Her experience with volcanoes and glaciers, which even included waterfall ice climbing, was valuable, but she recognized that the requirements had changed. Dillingham described the implications of this change as follows:

> In Washington I had been involved in mostly sandstone climbing. Here in Colorado it is mostly granite. As such, I had to spruce up what I could do in terms of technical rock climbing. There is a grading system for technical rock. Once you pull out the ropes and start using them on rocks, the grading system starts at 5.0 and it goes up to 5.13. In terms of my ability, I had never gotten above leading 5.9. So, I shifted to doing more rock climbing while I was out here. Nothing I've done before was of such major proportion and demand, involving all the gear and preplanning, as was Mt. Kongur in China. Every bit of preparation and effort toward meeting the technical requirements was worth it.

The extent to which standards are de-intellectualized and made concrete and behavioral will usually determine the extent to which the standard can be performed. It is not enough to require that team members have a "good attitude," or "be committed," or "put a lot of effort into their work." While such statements of standards are worthwhile and even noble, they tell you very little about the specific, behavioral performance that is required. During our interview with Tom Quinn, he described how the standards of performance required of the defensive backs on the 1966 Notre Dame championship football team were made concrete and understandable.

> We had something called "hamburger drill." It was a great metaphor. We had guys about 20 or 30 yards apart. There were about 8 of us defensive backs on one side and about 36 running backs down on the other end. In the middle there were a couple of linemen. These two guys would beat the shit out of each other. Then, a running back would

run as fast as he could, and the defensive back would try to tackle him. Now, when the head of a defensive back hits an offensive back's knees and thighs, the defensive back is going to take a much greater brunt than the offensive back. Sometimes they would give us smelling salts after a hit, and it would be enough to wake us up. We would stagger back out there and do it again. We ended up with two or three guys left, and they kept us. I guess it showed them who had the mental and physical toughness. Probably more mental than anything else.

Forgetting for the moment whether or not Tom Quinn's description of the "hamburger drill" appeals to our personal sense of values, the performance standard required of the defensive backs—mental and physical stamina—was articulated in a demonstrable fashion. It was never unclear what was expected of the defensive backs during a game.

The result of this clear understanding of the standard, and the subsequent effort required during its implementation, was observed at the end of Notre Dame's 1966 championship season. The defense was so good that only 38 points were scored on Notre Dame that entire year. But the standards of excellence were not unique to the defensive unit. The offense gave up only 14 errors the entire season. In fact, 60 minutes of play during scheduled games is required to qualify for a varsity letter. The offense was so good that at the end of the season, star wide receiver Jim Seymour barely qualified for a varsity letter with 62 minutes of play for the entire season logged into the game book.

It should be apparent by now that the execution of standards does not simply occur; it is highly dependent upon two ingredients. The first is a concrete understanding of the performance requirements necessary for success. The need for such clarity is perhaps most obvious in situations in which there are immediate consequences for good or poor adherence to standards. Examples are mountain-climbing teams, or football teams, or cardiac surgery teams, or any other effort in which there is pressure to perform within a limited amount of time. However, the need for clear and concrete standards is also great in those situations in which performance requirements or responsibilities tend to be ambiguous, such as on executive management teams where there is more freedom of choice in the execution of responsibilities. It is arguable that because of the inherent ambiguity in these situations, the need to clarify standards is even greater.

The second ingredient necessary for the execution of standards requires little elaboration. Once standards are defined, it is usually a matter of effort and hard work. To that end, standards require *discipline*.

STANDARDS ARE EASY TO IGNORE

Anyone who has ever attempted to make a positive change in his or her lifestyle knows how tempting and easy it is to ignore a standard. Whether the lifestyle change involves better nutritional habits, no tobacco, less alcohol, or more daily exercise, one quickly comes to grips with the fact that there are many equally appealing choices in the world, and the sustainability of standards requires constant vigilance.

An example of such vigilance occurred toward the completion of the Boeing 747 project, as Joe Sutter, chief engineer, recalled:

> There are always internal politics in a big organization. There were some people who wanted to fly the airplane on December 17, the Wright brothers' anniversary. But the airplane was a month or two away with all of the functional tests necessary to get it ready. It's a big limber airplane. We had to go through the high speed test carefully. It might take us a month because we were worried about flutter.

It's easy to understand how appealing it would be to coordinate the maiden voyage of the 747, the largest and most advanced airplane in the world, with the Wright brothers' anniversary. Seeing and feeling the appeal of having these two significant events share the same anniversary date does not mean that one has taken leave of his or her senses. However, as Sutter pointed out, if Boeing did not emphasize the technical standards established for the project over the historical value of a December 17 maiden flight, then it would not have been fulfilling some key responsibilities. The issue in this case, to the nonevaluative eye, is not whether the 747 should or shouldn't have had its test flight on December 17. This example is not one of a good decision versus a bad decision, or right versus wrong. Rather it is an example of how easy it is to find appealing reasons to challenge well-developed and systematically established standards. In such cases, if standards are to be either adhered to, or reasonably and fairly reexamined, then vigilance and fortitude are required. If there are reasons for establishing standards, then there should be reasons for not discarding them easily. Conversely, it would not be difficult to argue that standards that are easily discarded were never really standards at all.

Sometimes standards are ignored in more subtle ways than the brief, but powerful, contention created by the appearance of equally appealing choices. Sometimes standards outlive their usefulness and need to be recalibrated—as the U.S. Navy discovered at two critical times in its history. The first occurred during the Vietnam War, as Captain Joe Prueher, eventual developer and first commander of the U.S. Navy Strike Warfare Center, described:

> We lost about 16 fighter planes during fighter missions in Vietnam, and the Air Force lost a bunch also. As a result of that, the Navy formed Top Gun, and the Air Force created the Air Force Tactical Fighter Weapon School, which is at Nellis Air Force Base. We realized we weren't doing as well with air-to-air fighter tactics as we ought to be doing.

The second example contains a bit of a different twist. While the Vietnam lesson focused on individual fighter tactics, the lesson that followed the Beirut incident of 1983—in which the United States made an unsuccessful retaliatory strike against terrorists—centered on coordinated strategies and tactics of a much larger scale. Captain Prueher talked about the need to improve this coordinated tactical standard and how this need led to the creation of the U.S. Navy Strike Warfare Center in Fallon, Nevada:

> Within the Navy, the carrier battle group is the centerpiece. The carrier battle group has an aircraft carrier, it has other support ships, it has an airwing of about 85 airplanes on it, and it also has a couple of submarines. That is the unit that travels together to go around as an instrument of our policy. Sometimes we bring two carrier battle groups together. For example, we have two carrier battle groups in the Mediterranean most of the time.
>
> The linchpin of the carrier battle group is what those airplanes do for projecting power. It's the visible part, and it should be the most effective part of our national power. When we rang the bell in Beirut in 1983, it just didn't work as well as it might have for a variety of rea-

sons. . . . So, what we were after was trying to make the airwing strike capability and the battle group capability as good as it can possibly be.

The way Top Gun works is they take individuals and teach them the mechanics of fighting an individual airplane. They work in multisets of airplanes too, but that's strictly air-to-air. That's a subset of what we're trying to do at the Strike Warfare Center. The Top Gun people come up, and we integrate them into our effort at Strike Warfare. We're working coordinated tactics, where we integrate intelligence, what the people on the ground are doing, our air-to-ground attack, the fighter cover, and the strike escort, which is what Top Gun teaches, and so forth.

At Strike Warfare, we focus on a ground school curriculum, airwing training, and tactics development. Much of it is intact group training. The airwing, a group of airplanes on a ship, deploy en masse to Fallon, which we try to treat like a ship in the middle of the desert.

It might have been easy for the Navy to explain the loss of fighter planes during the Vietnam War as the "cost of doing business." And, it might have been equally as easy to explain the Beirut incident as a "long shot." It might have been easy, in other words, to become defensive about performance. Instead, the Navy chose to view both of those experiences as feedback regarding performance standards. They were opportunities to reexamine, as objectively as possible, a fundamental framework of standards that had been established for achieving results and then make any necessary improvements.

Maintaining standards is a constant, vigilant activity, requiring effort and fortitude. No matter how appealing the immediate alternative might be, a well-established standard should be given due attention before it is allowed to be relaxed. Likewise, when ignored or left unexamined, standards will deteriorate over time.

THREE COMMON FEATURES OF STANDARDS OF EXCELLENCE

Our research findings generated three variables that appear integral to establishing and sustaining standards of excellence. The extent to which these variables are present determines HOW a team pursues success.

First, it is necessary to establish a set of standards which embrace several others variables: individual commitment, motivation, self-esteem, and, certainly, performance. Needless to say, the extent to which standards are clearly and concretely articulated determines the eventual likelihood of the standards being met.

Second, it's important for individual team members to require one another to perform according to the established standards of excellence. The only way a standard is sustained is through its performance. The seriousness and worth of any standard eventually boils down to each individual's support of the standard as demonstrated by the amount of effort invested in meeting it. Individual performance is the best method for sustaining standards of excellence.

Third, it's important for a team to exert pressure on itself to make those changes constantly that improve performance standards. Our research sample clearly indicates that successful teams do not allow themselves to rest on the laurels of past performance. On the contrary, successful teams never become satisfied with how well they've done. They actively work at ways of finding reasons to be dissatisfied with their performance. Each performance is an opportunity to discover ways of doing it better next time.

In summary, standards of excellence consist of pressure to perform. While pressure may be exerted in several different ways, it is eventually focused on individual effort, as team performance is ultimately dependent upon how each individual executes assigned responsibilities. Without question, standards make a difference in the eventual performance of a team. While standards are hard work and easy to ignore, the rewards, both tangible and intangible, are monumental.

8

External Support and Recognition

External support and recognition is a somewhat "fuzzy" factor used by the interviewees to differentiate high- and low-success teams. Typical markers signaling the presence of external support and recognition include the following: The team is given the resources it needs to get the job done. The team is supported by those individuals and agencies outside the team who are capable of contributing to the team's success. The team is sufficiently recognized for its accomplishments. And the reward and incentive structure is clear, viewed as appropriate by team members, and tied to performance.

Interestingly, the "external support and recognition factor" seems to be more an effect of team success than a cause of it. It is noted more for its absence in poorly functioning teams than for its presence in effective ones. Because it is a less well-defined factor in this research, as well as in the literature on teams, we are prepared to make only four assertions about this factor.

1. EXTERNAL SUPPORT AND RECOGNITION ARE IMPORTANT

Some social scientists have alluded to the "invisible team," people outside of the team who have expectations of it and make demands on it (Hastings, Bixby, & Chaudry-Lawton, 1987). Although these people may not be a part of the infrastructure that supports the team, they may relate to the team in important ways, as do the fans of a sports team, the community within which a disaster team operates, and the media who occasionally interact with an epidemiology team. Thus, the external support and recognition that are often important to the team may involve constituencies beyond the specific organization of which the team is a part.

A number of well-regarded researchers and practitioners, identifying factors such as individuals being rewarded/compensated on the basis of the team's effectiveness, team members being provided with the necessary resources to do the job, and people in positions of power supporting the ideas and actions of teams, substantiate the significance of external support to team success (Hollingsworth, Meglino, & Shaner, 1979; Likert, 1976; Dyer, 1977).

The belief that external support and recognition is an important ingredient in team success extends to the sample of team leaders and members we interviewed. This belief is also held by the intact teams we have investigated and consulted with in phase three of our research, described in Chapter 10.

2. THE ABSENCE OF EXTERNAL SUPPORT AND RECOGNITION IS NOTICED MORE THAN ITS PRESENCE

Dr. Michael Gregg, discussing epidemiology teams out of the Centers for Disease Control, stated:

> I'm sure there are other attributes that, when they are not there, cause problems. If you are looking at the kind of team efforts that we have been discussing, namely, sending people out to do investigations for you, we cannot forget the support from the people back home. You just can't let a team go out there and expect it to go by itself. You've got to have a relatively strong umbilical cord from the team back to home base. Any team that is working out of its normal environment needs first-rate support, supervisors who will be on call 24 hours a day, who are understanding, willing to listen, and know how to communicate. They've got to have experience in the field so they can identify with the problems the field team is having, in order to be useful at all. They've got to provide the kind of services that will make a field team feel that it is not isolated or on its own.

When the support is not there, there are problems. The problems frequently involve the loss of morale, the erosion of confidence, increased feelings of helplessness and futility and, sometimes, even a decreased belief in and commitment to the team's goal. It can be difficult indeed to view the goal as significant when important others, through their behavior, convey the view that the goal is relatively unimportant.

Team leaders and members tend to notice the absence of support. Joe Sutter, leader of the Boeing 747 Project team, said that the only two teams he recalled that had special and prolonged difficulties did not have the support of top management.

> They could sense that even upper management wasn't behind the project. There were a lot of guys in upper management who thought the program was going to go belly-up. So, the guys were working with the feeling that, "I'm working on something my boss isn't even interested in."

We've said that the absence of external support and recognition gets noticed much more frequently than its presence. In fact, support and recognition is more likely to become an issue for a team under two specific conditions: (1) when it's doing very poorly and (2) when it's doing very well. A considerable body of social science research on teams, recently synthesized by Coleman (1987), discloses an interesting pattern: When teams do well or win, success is attributed to factors within the team itself; when teams do poorly or lose, such failing team performance is usually attributed to factors outside—presumably beyond the control and blame of the team.

So at the *low end* of the performance continuum, teams are likely to see less external support than is *necessary to achieve the goal*. At the *high end*, on the other hand, teams are slightly more likely to perceive less support and recognition than is *warranted by the achievement*. In other words, when teams are doing well in the other categories identified by our research, then there is a slightly higher tendency for them to identify a problem in the external support and recognition category. This pattern also appeared in our monitoring of ongoing teams during the third phase of our research, reported in Chapter 10. This heightened sensitivity about support and recognition, under conditions of either success or failure, leads to the third statement we feel confident in making.

3. TANGIBLE SUPPORT LAGS BEHIND PHILOSOPHICAL
SUPPORT

In Chapter 1 we reviewed some evidence—both cultural trends and individual cases—of philosophical support for the concept of teams and guarded optimism about what teams may be capable of achieving. Still, this attitudinal support for teams and team concepts seems uncomfortably out-of-step with many aspects of organizational reality. One observer of this inconsistency between attitude and structural support wrote that:

> spirit and teamwork are most difficult to create. A big part of the problem in most organizations is that there are no teams. Managers call for teamwork from their people, but without identifying any team except the entire organization; and the entire organization is usually so large or complex that employees cannot identify with it. The whole organization can rarely be a team. (Sherwin, 1976, p. 158)

Earlier we observed that when teams are formed, they either identify by themselves, or are confronted with, a clear and elevating goal, and then they are frequently left to operate within a structure that is simply a by-product of other considerations. Dyer (1977) has warned that for team-building programs to work, people in positions of power must support changes, and some of these changes must be structural, such as performance reviews, raises, and promotions. Along the same lines, it has been argued that:

> top management must demonstrate its commitment to a number of difficult changes: in work design, in organizational structure, and in information and measurement systems, to name just a few. There must be a reward system that recognizes team effort and values people's input to the team, and there must be performance appraisal of the team as a team. (Galagan, 1986, p. 35)

There is clear evidence that organizations are making the structural changes alluded to by Dyer. One new source recently reviewed performance plans across a variety of organizations and concluded that "group-based," including team-based, incentive systems are being recommended increasingly by compensation experts and that consultants estimate that group plans will grow at twice the rate of individual plans ("Grading," 1988). Another news source reported an array of cases in which team outcomes are being achieved by organizations that are designing teamwork into the organizational structures (Keidel, 1988).

Reducing the discrepancy between the *philosophical support for the concept of teams* and the *structural support provided real teams* is worthwhile for several reasons. First, there is considerable social scientific evidence that collaborative or cooperative efforts generate higher levels of achievement *across the group as a whole* than do individual or competitive efforts (e.g., Kohn, 1986). Our research strongly supports this conclusion. In fact, we have already reviewed two complementary conclusions: (1) Intense collaboration within the group is associated with high performance or successful groups; (2) competitive climates and the pursuit of individual agendas within the group are factors associated with low performance or unsuccessful groups.

The second reason for realigning structures to fit the philosophical concept of teams more closely is that such changes increase the likelihood of intense loyalties to the organizations making the changes. Sociologists Peter and Patricia Adler (in press) have amassed convincing evidence that: (1) Intense loyalty is greater in organizations where productivity is achieved on a group basis rather than by individual achievement; (2) intense loyalty is greater in organizations that are structured so that individuals are dependent on the success of the group for their own success. Thus, there are good reasons to believe that structural changes in the direction of support for "team concepts" might have a positive impact on two very important keys to collective success—achievement and loyalty.

As we've already indicated in our discussion of team structure, teams themselves must be designed so that their structural features are consistent with the broad objectives of the team (problem-solving, creativity, tactical execution). However, with respect to the structural features of the broader organization within which the team operates, we believe we have identified one structural change that would probably improve the success of most, if not all, teams. This one change arises from the most frequent theme in those interviews that identified external support and recognition as a factor associated with team success.

4. THE MOST BASIC STRUCTURAL CHANGE INVOLVES TANGIBLE REWARDS

To keep things in perspective, let's return to an earlier point. The first conclusion we stated about teams is that if the goal is clear and also worthwhile, challenging, or personally elevating, then all kinds of other issues become secondary. Lon McCain, chief financial officer of Petro-Lewis Corporation, captured the spirit of that conclusion particularly well describing conditions just before the oil crash:

> The deadlines were grueling in a lot of ways, and there were times when we would work around the clock, sometimes for two or three days in a row, or we would work 20-hour days and get two or three hours of sleep and come back and repeat that over and over again for a week or more. When we were doing the royalty trust, it was almost three months. It's grueling, but it also builds up your adrenaline when you know you are going to hit your deadline even though it is going to be tight, and it feels like fun. The royalty trust was an extraordinary transaction, and we would have 50 people at the printer's, people in different rooms writing and negotiating and going through different parts of the disclosure documents, people trying to write the basic documents that would set out the terms and the conditions of the deal. It wasn't a party atmosphere, but something close to that. People didn't drink, but we got giddy anyway because we got tired. People were making jokes; then there would be a lull; someone would bring in Chinese food. It's just sort of a camaraderie. People feel like they're going through something together.

When a team is in pursuit of a goal, especially a challenging or significant one, other considerations tend to fade into the background. But when that "sense of urgency" is not so compelling as to overshadow everything else, then external support and recognition becomes a consideration. As you might expect, the factor most consistently identified with external support and recognition is money—whether it comes in the form of compensation, or reward, or incentive.

In addition to the enjoyment of the work, Lon McCain talked about the money factor:

> The other reward was the financial reward. People got bonuses. We paid them for working hard. The general compensation level was al-

ready above average, so everybody always thought they were being treated well to begin with. But we also had benefit plans they enjoyed that other people didn't.

Tangible rewards are important. But tangible rewards by themselves don't necessarily contribute to team success. For example, in our discussion of unified commitment, we reviewed a number of cases in which too heavy an emphasis on individual objectives can interfere with team success. So the tangible rewards, though individual, need to be tied to collective success. When Duke Drake took over Dun and Bradstreet in 1975, his first priority was to build a team to run the company from the top. Drake's first principle in building that team was to select the right people. His second principle was to make sure that the incentives were clearly understood. "That's one base it's important to touch. I told people what they could expect to earn, given a set of assumptions about how the company itself would grow." Drake made sure that this initial team understood that they would not only share in the decision making, but they would share in the consequences of those decisions: "This stuff about lonely at the top is a bunch of B.S. If you're lonely at the top you're not doing your job."

The need to integrate objectives at a higher level and to move some incentives up to a group level is also recognized by Charles F. Knight, CEO of Emerson Electric: "We have already built some incentives that are tied to the collective effort. Regardless of what happens to a particular unit, a manager may profit or not profit by what the collective does."

No one in our sample went so far as to recommend compensating an entire team and then allowing the team to make decisions about the distribution of that compensation to its individual members. Granted, professional sports teams have been employing a version of such a plan for handling bonus compensation earned through extraordinary achievement by the team, such as winning a championship or surviving in a playoff series. But the organizational structure supporting teams in nonsports contexts still relies on individual compensation plans. The closest we got to a team compensation plan were suggestions from several interviewees which, in the aggregate, would take the following form:

Step 1. Identify a standard tangible enough to allow for the measurement of some relevant dimension of a team's performance. Some hypothetical examples:

A. Given this kind of construction project, in this geographic location, at this time of year, and this projected time to completion, we should expect to lose 350 person-hours of working time to personal injury.

B. Given this product being manufactured, this fabrication process, this set of specifications, and this rate of production, we would expect 22% of the chips to be scrap.

C. Given this volume of calls received as customer complaints, during this period of time, on this range of services or products, we expect to find 1.8% of the cases recorded as transferred to our legal department.

Step 1, then, involves working out, in as concrete terms as possible, a relevant performance standard for the team.

Step 2. Identify a range within which that performance standard may be expected to vary. The range should be a reasonable one because if a goal is regarded by the team as unreasonable or impossible to attain, the performance is more likely to decline than to improve. Let's say the process of arriving at these ranges has involved at least the team leader and makes sense to the team. Then it would be possible to continue the illustration with ranges such as:

A. 80% of the time we can expect the person-hours lost to personal injury to range between 320 and 380.

B. 90% of the time, on a monthly basis, we can expect the percentage of units produced that are scrapped to range between 17% and 28%.

C. Almost always, on a quarterly basis, the percentage of complaint calls going from customer relations to legal ranges between 1.6% and 2%.

In Step 2 you attempt to set a new performance standard which is (1) reasonable to the team, (2) clear evidence of team achievement, and (3) unlikely to be attributable to fluctuations in other contributing factors.

Step 3. Set the compensation the team will receive for achieving a new performance standard.

A. 320 person-hours lost to personal injury is a reasonable goal for this project. The difference, in real cost to the company, of the number of hours actually lost and the 320 projected will be returned to the team to use or distribute as it sees fit. The company will take its benefits in reduced insurance premiums in the future, clients that are more satisfied by virtue of an earlier completion of the project, and the knowledge that fewer of their people were hurt on the job.

B. In some customized chip manufacturing processes, where it is not unusual for each scrap unit to represent manufacturing costs of approximately $1,000 per unit, the amount of money saved by a substantial reduction in waste could be considerable. Even a small but significant share of these savings could serve as a clear, challenging, and rewarding goal for a fabrication team.

C. If we monitor the increased costs of settling X number of complaints in customer relations, and the decreased costs associated with resolving those complaints in the legal department, this cost difference will vary as a function of the difference between the projected percentage of cases going to legal and the new performance standard we achieve in customer relations. Customer relations will receive 25% of those savings to use or distribute as it sees fit.

As logical as this approach to compensating teams might seem, problems associated with it always surfaced quickly in our discussions of ways to reward team performance. First, you would have to institute guarantees that the new performance standard was not attained by somehow compromising quality standards in some other area of the team's activity. For example, the reduction in waste could not be achieved by allowing defective units somehow to escape the quality control process. Second, you would have to institute guarantees that new performance standards could not be attained simply by allowing performance to deteriorate to the point where, subsequently, new performance standards could be attained relatively easily.

Whatever the problems that would need attention and resolution, we encountered agreement on two points relative to comments falling into the category of "external support and recognition." First, for team concepts really to impact the performance levels of groups and teams engaged in more routine activities, some organizational design changes, especially in the area of financial rewards, must occur. Second, given the value we have traditionally placed on individual achievement and our practice of compensating individual performance, we probably do not fully appreciate the levels of performance teams could reach if they were not only in pursuit of a worthwhile goal, but also *rewarded* as a team for *behaving* as a team.

9

Principled Leadership

The final ingredient in effective team performance—and one of the most critical—is team leadership. Our research strongly indicates that the right person in a leadership role can add tremendous value to any collective effort, even to the point of sparking the outcome with an intangible kind of magic.

For example, leaders can turn around an undesirable situation, as did Ara Parseghian, who as head coach of the Notre Dame football team during the 1965 and 1966 seasons took a mediocre team and turned it into a national champion. Leaders can motivate a team to follow them through the most rigorous of standards and grueling efforts, as exemplified by pioneering heart surgeons Michael DeBakey and Denton Cooley. And they can be instrumental in changing priorities and generating support for ideas and programs, as did Dr. Alex Langmuir of the Centers for Disease Control, who saved the polio vaccination program from extinction after a defective vaccine infected a small number of children and threatened to end this entire lifesaving effort.

A CONSISTENT MESSAGE

We are certainly not the first to study the role of leaders. The importance of leadership and its conspicuous absence in a multitude of contexts has been described, discussed, and debated for several years now. Some recent views even suggest that the element of leadership has received far more attention than it deserves (Kiechel, 1988).

Generally, however, writers and researchers of the past decade have concentrated on the need for leadership to focus on the relationships among three elements: the goal or vision, how to cause change to occur, and how best to involve followers. A consistent and well-focused point of view has begun to emerge.

The genesis of such thinking began with James MacGregor Burns in his seminal 1978 book, *Leadership*, in which he distinguished the transactional leader from the transforming leader as follows:

> The relations of most leaders and followers are transactional—leaders approach followers with an eye to exchanging one thing for another: jobs for votes, or subsidies for campaign contributions. Such transactions comprise the bulk of the relationships among leaders and followers. . . . Transforming leadership, while more complex, is more potent. . . . The transforming leader looks for potential motives and followers, seeks to satisfy higher needs, and engages the full person of the follower. The result of transforming leadership is a relationship of mutual stimulation and elevation that converts followers into leaders and may convert leaders into moral agents. (p. 4)

From this conceptually rigorous perspective, Burns referred to Gandhi as perhaps the best modern example of a transforming leader, someone "who aroused and elevated the hopes and demands of millions of Indians and whose life and personality were enhanced in the process" (p. 20). Finally, Burns placed a stake in the ground regarding the true test of such leadership when he defined leadership as "the achievement of significant change that represents the collective interests of leaders and followers" (p. 251).

Following Burns and his change-agent perspective, equally cogent thinkers further developed the concept of leadership as transformation. Charles Kiefer and Peter Senge (1984) proffered the term *metanoic*, from a Greek word meaning "a fundamental shift of mind." The metanoic organization, according to Kiefer and Senge, is based upon the principle that individuals can have extraordinary influence once aligned with a common vision. The metanoic organization embraces five primary dimensions: (1) a deep sense of vision or purposefulness; (2) alignment around that vision; (3) empowering people; (4) structural integrity; and (5) the balance of reason and intuition (p. 111). Leaders, according to these five principles, are "responsible for sustaining vision, catalyzing alignment, and evolving policy and structure. They frequently conceive of themselves as teachers, but they do not control the system. Most don't even think it's possible to control an organization effectively from the top" (p. 119). Such leaders focus unusual attention on teaching employees how the organization and the business operate.

In 1985, Warren Bennis and Burt Nanus directly adopted Burns' notion, defining transformative leadership as follows: " . . . the new leader . . . is one who commits people to action, who converts followers into leaders, and who may convert leaders into agents of change. We refer to this as 'transformative leadership' " (p. 3).

Following interviews with 90 distinctive and successful leaders in various professions, Bennis and Nanus identified four primary components of the transformative leader: (1) creating attention through vision—creating a focus that is compelling and results-oriented; (2) creating meaning through communication—the capacity to relate a compelling image that is fostered through shared meanings, symbols, and images powerful enough to induce enthusiasm and commitment; (3) establishing trust through positioning—assuring that the leader's behavior exemplifies the ideals and course of the vision; and (4) the deployment of self through positive self-regard—"leadership is an essentially human business" (p. 55). Regarding the last point, Bennis and Nanus point out that "there was no trace of self-worship or cockiness in our leaders" (p. 57).

During the next three years, three thoughtful efforts continued to contribute to and expand this line of thinking. In 1986, Tichy and Devanna's book, *The Transformational Leader*, emphasized three leadership skills: First, the leader must recognize the need for revitalization and change of some sort; second, the leader must create a vision that depicts how things might be different in the future if the change occurs; and third, the leader must institutionalize change so that it will survive the leader's tenure (pp. 5–6).

In 1987, *The Renewal Factor*, by Robert Waterman, built upon the work he and Tom Peters began a few years earlier in their 1982 *In Search of Excellence*, by looking at people as sources of organizational renewal. Based on a research effort that included an in-depth study of 45 organizations that had "renewed" themselves, Waterman emphasized that leaders in renewing organizations brought a stabilizing factor by constantly reminding people that change is normal and inevitable, and should be valued (p. 233). The vision portion of the renewing company, according to Waterman, is provided by leaders who are able to find a way to give people a sense of pride that will result in a sense of commitment (p. 242).

Finally, John Kotter, in his 1988 book, *The Leadership Factor*, advanced the overall concept of leadership by describing some of the attributes necessary for success. Based on interviews with 150 managers from 40 firms; questionnaire data from nearly 1,000 top-level executives; the examination of best practices in 15 corporations; and an in-depth analysis of how five corporations attracted, developed, and retained leadership talent, Kotter observed that, at the broadest level, leaders focus on (1) an intelligent agenda for change and then (2) build a strong, energized network of necessary resources (p. 19). Kotter's contribution also included the identification of some necessary requirements for effective leadership: (1) industry and organizational knowledge; (2) solid relationships in the firm and industry; (3) an excellent reputation and a strong track record; (4) abilities and skills that include a keen mind and strong interpersonal skills; (5) personal values that broadly appreciate all peoples and groups; and (6) the ability to motivate through high energy and a strong desire to lead (p. 30).

Although reflecting several different perspectives, such insightful thinkers have converged on three consistent characteristics of leadership. Effective leaders (1) establish a vision; (2) create change; and (3) unleash talent. Our research findings were consistent with these cumulative findings of the past decade.

First, we found that effective team leaders begin by establishing a vision of the future. The observable consensus across our interviews was that team leaders have a vision of the way something could and should be. In the most common language of our sample of interviewees, this need was articulated as the clear, elevating goal described in Chapter 2. Such a goal, or vision, is a hallmark of effective leaders. They articulate what an organization can and should become, or what a team can or should accomplish. Furthermore, they articulate the team's goal in such a way as to inspire a desire for and eventual commitment to the accomplishment of the goal. The goal, or vision, is seen as worthwhile, making team members eager to be a part of its achievement.

Vernon R. Loucks, chairman and CEO of Baxter International, described this aspect of leadership as "the highest form of commitment. This is accomplished when people want to do their best because senior management has helped them understand what really must happen—short- and long-term—in order for the business to be successful."

Second, effective leaders create change. They influence movement

away from the status quo. As early Greek and Latin etymology suggests, the word *leadership* is derived from the verb to act, to begin, to
set in motion.[1] Effective leaders intuitively recognize the obvious:
The vision of the way things could be is different from the way things
are now, and this requires someone to cause changes to occur. The
effectiveness of this perspective, according to our findings, is in the
leader's ability to demonstrate to team members that change is possible. Effective leaders have a plan or an agenda for change, and they
demonstrate that the plan is possible by demonstrating an ability to
make things happen. They are able to influence constituencies outside the team—for example, the next level of management, the
board, the media, the industry—to support the team's effort.

Third, effective team leaders unleash the energy and talents of
contributing members. They motivate team members to take an
action-oriented approach toward achieving the objective. It is within
the context of this dimension of leadership that our research data
yield an especially interesting and worthwhile observation.

A PERSPECTIVE FOR UNLEASHING TALENT

Here, it's important to note that in this chapter we are departing
from the anecdotal approach that served us well in previous chapters.
We are not convinced that the behaviors of specific leaders can be
generalized to other leaders. So rather than citing a litany of leaders
and describing how they performed, we undertook a content analysis
of our research data to identify the common behaviors of effective
and ineffective leaders. While our interview sample confirmed that
effective leaders establish clear, elevating goals and demonstrate the
ability to create the necessary changes that make goal achievement
possible, we became most interested in how team leaders unleash the
energy and talents of team members.

During the interviews we conducted, each interviewee was asked
to describe the qualities and behaviors of team leaders whom they
recalled as being unusually effective or successful. We asked them to
describe not only what those leaders did, but also what they con-
sciously avoided doing. We then asked about the interviewees' experiences with ineffective leaders and what they found particularly noteworthy.

A content analysis of our research data yielded a consistent message that focused on how team leaders generated enthusiasm, a bias for action, and a commitment to the team's objective among team members. The single most distinguishing feature of the effective leaders in our data base was their ability to establish, and lead by, guiding principles. These principles represented day-to-day performance standards. They represented what all team members, including the team leader, should expect from one another on a day-to-day basis.

The principles identified by our sample created three natural categories of expectations: (1) what the team should expect of the team leader; (2) what the team leader should expect from each team member, and each team member should expect from one another; and (3) leadership principles that established a supportive decision-making climate in which team members could take risks.

1. Team Leader

The first set of leadership principles that emerged from our data described what team members could expect of the team leader. These principles were most commonly described in the form of the following six expectations:

As team leader, I will:
1. Avoid compromising the team's objective with political issues.
2. Exhibit personal commitment to our team's goal.
3. Not dilute the team's efforts with too many priorities.
4. Be fair and impartial toward all team members.
5. Be willing to confront and resolve issues associated with inadequate performance by team members.
6. Be open to new ideas and information from team members.

The effective leaders described by our sample were characterized by their adherence to a dependable set of values. They were, if you will, "principled" about their approach toward accomplishment and how they would conduct themselves along the way.

2. Team Members

The second set of principles described what the team leader could expect from each team member and, correspondingly, what team members should expect from each other. This set of principles placed responsibility on each team member to manage appropriately his or her membership within the group. The content analysis of our interview data generated the following 12 guiding principles:

Each team member will be expected to:
1. Demonstrate a realistic understanding of his/her role and accountabilities.
2. Demonstrate objective and fact-based judgments.
3. Collaborate effectively with other team members.
4. Make the team goal a higher priority than any personal objective.
5. Demonstrate a willingness to devote whatever effort is necessary to achieve team success.
6. Be willing to share information, perceptions, and feedback openly.
7. Provide help to other team members when needed and appropriate.
8. Demonstrate high standards of excellence.
9. Stand behind and support team decisions.
10. Demonstrate courage of conviction by directly confronting important issues.
11. Demonstrate leadership in ways which contribute to the team's success.
12. Respond constructively to feedback from others.

It is within the context of these 12 principles, or some variation of them, that the effective team leaders as described by our sample exhibited leadership excellence. Such principles created a value-driven leadership style, placing the responsibility for appropriate team behavior squarely in the lap of each team member.

In fact, the concept of leading by principles was the most distinguishing feature of the effective leaders described by our research sample. In each case, interviewees commented that the excellent leaders were very tough on principles, not on people. And the leaders made sure that there were real consequences if the principles were violated. After all, no consequences means no standards—which translates into very little leadership. Moreover, the establishment of such principles incorporated a basic respect for people, their abilities, their opportunities to achieve, and the relationship between their accomplishment and their self-esteem. At the same time, however, these principles established performance standards that created a relentless expectation to achieve the team goal. In effect, the leader managed the principles, and the principles managed the team.

LEADER

↓

PRINCIPLES

↓

TEAM

Our research findings regarding the role of "principled leadership" coincide with the natural but unsystematic emergence of this kind of thinking among progressive groups. More and more, in government, business, and social institutions, we are seeing the emergence of leadership that is focused on principles and values—on the belief that there are no shortcuts to "doing it right." Approaches to quality (Crosby, 1979), organizations devoted to exploring issues of ethics (The Center for Ethics and Corporate Policy, Chicago, IL), and the new concept of service guarantees (Hart, 1988) are all topical ways in which corporate leadership, in particular, is assuming its moral and professional responsibility to employees, customers, and suppliers.

3. Decision-Making Climate

The third set of leadership principles, and we believe the most important, clearly focused attention on the creation of a supportive decision-making climate. The effective leaders described by our sample created decision-making environments that unleashed people's willingness to exhibit a bias for action, which in turn created an enthusiasm and commitment to the team's objective. This was accomplished by giving team members the confidence to take risks, make choices, and actively contribute to the team's success.

Decision-making confidence was directly related to the principles established by the team leader. These principles served as guidelines for making choices. Effective leaders understood that excellence could only be achieved if all members were willing to make choices that resulted in actions and changes, thereby moving the team toward its objective. Effective leaders knew it was impossible to make all decisions themselves. They also knew that it was equally impossible, and certainly not desirable, to specify all decisions that would be made by each team member. However, it was possible to establish leadership principles that would encourage people to act confidently on their own. These principles encouraged team members to take risks, and to act, which, as we may recall from the etymology of the word itself, is the core of leadership. They created a value system that encouraged people to act confidently, rather than be concerned about doing the wrong thing. This fostered a decision-making climate that inspired team members to feel they had the power to act, to make choices, and to make a difference, rather than feel apprehensive of or superfluous to the end result.

The logic that emerged from our research regarding how important encouragement and support is to decision-making is simple and difficult to ignore:

- To achieve an elevated goal or vision, change must occur.
- For change to occur, a decision must be made.
- For a decision to occur, a choice must be made.
- To make a choice, a risk must be taken.
- To encourage risk-taking, a supportive climate must exist.
- A supportive climate is demonstrated by day-to-day leadership behavior.

According to our sample of interviewees, effective team leaders gave team members clear signals, which encouraged them to act. The leadership principles that created this supportive decision-making climate were most commonly demonstrated when the team leader lived up to the following five behaviors:

As team leader, I will provide a supportive decision-making climate by:
1. Trusting team members with meaningful levels of responsibility.
2. Providing team members the necessary autonomy to achieve results.
3. Presenting challenging opportunities which stretch the individual abilities of team members.
4. Recognizing and rewarding superior performance.
5. Standing behind our team and supporting it.

These five principles were identified repeatedly as playing an important role in unleashing the best abilities of other people. Such principles were seen as encouraging people to become involved, to act, and to make decisions because they establish a climate that is fair and appropriate. These principles encourage people to feel they are valued because they are given responsibilities, and trusted because they are given the necessary freedom to make decisions. They afford opportunities to grow; foster a belief that people's efforts will be recognized; and give team members the assurance that the team leader will be supportive of their efforts, and not leave them "hanging out to dry."

This type of a decision-making climate was described, in one way or another, as playing an integral part in bringing out the best in team members. In fact, each of the CEOs we interviewed identified a supportive decision-making climate as absolutely critical to the success of a team.

If we stop and think, we quickly realize, perhaps even recall from personal experience, that introducing change is a monumental task in and of itself. By definition, change requires a shifting away from the comfort of the status quo. This is usually when the antibodies come out and resist any effort to "do it differently." The effort required just to overcome such inertia is enormous. Now, add to this already difficult effort a climate that does not support people in exercising their best judgment. Is it any wonder people become uninterested, apprehensive, and risk-averse?

On the other hand, our data strongly suggest that a leadership climate that encourages and supports people taking risks and making choices will unleash a personal interest in the outcome. It's extremely difficult to invest one's personal judgment, which is what the opportunity to make decisions is all about, and not take a keen interest in the outcome of the effort. As Elliot Richardson, a man who has observed the principles of leadership as a member of five Presidential Cabinets, commented: "You cannot immerse yourself in work without getting interested in it." Such is the nature of a climate that encourages people to act.

EGO SUPPRESSION

Such an orientation, however, requires a constant suppression of the individual ego on behalf of all team members, beginning with the team leader. As Fiedler and Chemers (1974) observed, "Leadership is an amazingly ego-involving activity" (p. 5). It's all too easy for the "leadership role" to include, inherently, the presumptuous belief that judgment is more sound at the leader's level. It is the uncontrolled ego that can all too frequently get in the way of effective leadership. It can cause us to organize in convoluted configurations; venture into "interesting" business opportunities we have no business being in; hire people who should not be part of the team; and keep people who should be let go. Such ego-involvement is perhaps most apparent and potentially problematic, as Sonnenfeld (1988) recently observed, when leaders such as CEOs retire from their leadership position. As Quickel (1988) points out, it can also be an important factor when they try to select a successor.

LEADERS CREATE LEADERS

The most effective leaders, as reported by our sample, were those who subjugated their ego needs in favor of the team's goal. They allowed team members to take an active part in shaping the destiny of the team's effort. They allowed them to decide, to make choices, to act, to do something meaningful. The result of this approach was the creation of the "multiplier effect." It created a contagion among team members to unlock their own leadership abilities.

Whether it was in the context of college or professional football, mountain climbing, cardiac surgery, project teams, or executive management teams, the following observation held true: Effective leaders bring out the leadership in others. Effective leaders give team members the self-confidence to act, to take charge of their responsibilities, and make changes occur rather than merely perform assigned tasks. In short, leaders create leaders!

This is quite similar to Garfield's finding in his 1986 review of peak performers. Following interviews and discussions with more than 500 top performers, he concluded that peak-performing "team builders" develop and use three major skills: delegating to empower people to act, stretching the abilities of others, and encouraging educated risk-taking (pp. 31,181). At a more conceptual level, it is very similar to what Zaleznick (1977) posited as one of the primary differences between the focus of a manager and that of a leader: "The distinction is simply between a manager's attention to *how* things get done and a leader's to *what* the events and decisions mean to participants" (p. 73).

The payoff for providing a supportive decision-making climate is the level of confidence that spreads among team members. If the team leader is supportive. it is likely to foster similar support among team members. After all, no one wants to fail, or feel rejected, or feel his or her peers are constantly second-guessing each decision. That type of climate guarantees risk-aversion, hesitation, and indecision. Protect self-esteem at all cost! A supportive climate, on the other hand, lessens those possibilities by encouraging team members to take a risk, exhibit judgment, and make something happen. According to our results, that is when truly effective leadership begins to emerge—when team members become leaders themselves.

Leadership is clearly more than just putting "spin" on team effort. Effective leadership does, in fact, fundamentally change what the team effort is all about. Leaders make people feel connected with the mainstream of what is happening by helping them understand the organization's vision. By overcoming inertia, they demonstrate that change is possible. Perhaps most important, they create self-confidence in people, thereby encouraging them to take risks, make decisions, and act—in short, to be leaders themselves.

NOTE

1. Jennings. E. E. (1960). *An anatomy of leadership* (p. 3). New York: Harper & Brothers. Expanded upon from the descriptive research of Hannah Arendt (1958) in *The human condition* (pp. 188 ff.). Chicago: University of Chicago Press.

10

Inside Management Teams

The first stage of our research was undertaken to discover what the characteristics of effectively functioning teams might be. In the process, we discovered and defined eight properties of successful teams, which we then used as the basis for assessing the effectiveness of 32 management teams. For this purpose, we developed a feedback instrument that assesses the extent to which an intact team, as described by its leader and members, possesses or does not possess the characteristics we outlined in the preceding eight chapters. The information and insights generated by the feedback instrument were discussed during feedback sessions with each of the 32 teams. The feedback sessions were both intensive (face-to-face dialogues with intact teams), and extensive (each session lasting about six to 12 hours). Our ultimate goal, of course, was to develop a system that would allow any team to monitor and improve its own performance. In the remainder of this chapter we'll describe what we learned from this process.

THREE TYPES OF INFORMATION ABOUT THE 32 TEAMS

To provide a better feel for the kinds of conclusions we're going to report later in this chapter, let us briefly identify the nature of these teams.

First, they are teams that were interested in examining their own functioning. With rare exceptions, they asked to be assessed. The typical process involved a team leader, member, or higher-level manager who had somehow learned of our research and requested an assessment/feedback session. Therefore, the first thing to keep in mind is that the group is composed overwhelmingly of teams that are motivated to examine their own processes systematically and to seek ways to improve their performance. As we pointed out earlier, this self-assessment tendency is much more likely to characterize high performance teams. Thus, these 32 management teams are probably above average in effectiveness, and their scores on many of the data points we will discuss later seem to support this judgment.

Second, these are predominantly senior level management teams. The sizes of the organizations they represent vary dramatically, from some of the largest corporations in the United States to some very small, privately-owned companies. Nevertheless, the teams tend to be at or near the top of the organizational hierarchies.

Third, the teams are roughly balanced between operations and staff. Nineteen are operations teams—predominantly executive management; and 13 are staff teams—predominantly finance, human resources, and legal functions.

Finally, the teams are predominantly from manufacturing organizations (about 80%) and secondarily from service organizations (about 20%). We have accumulated three kinds of information on these 32 management teams.

1. Responses to scaled items. With the eight properties of effectively functioning teams as the primary categories, a set of items was written that represented the dominant themes within each category. These items were refined by a professional social science research organization, pilot-tested on a small sample of management team members, and then tested for internal consistency, by category, through an analysis of the responses of 128 management team members to the final set of items.[1]

The items were scaled in such as way as to allow a respondent to describe his or her team by comparing the team with a criterion that had emerged from our research. For example, some of the items are:

- Team members possess the essential skills and abilities to accomplish the team's objectives.
- Achieving our team goal is a higher priority than any individual objective.
- There are clear consequences connected with our team's success or failure in achieving our goal.
- Our communication system has opportunities for team members to raise issues not on the formal agenda.

Items such as these were rated by team leaders and members in terms of whether each item was judged true, more true than false, more false than true, or false when describing the team.

Three basic instruments were used to collect responses: (1) a booklet in which each team member recorded his/her description of the team; (2) a booklet in which the team leader recorded his/her description of the team; (3) a booklet in which the team member recorded his/her description of the extent to which each other member of the team contributed to the team's success. This information was collected from the team leaders and a total of 302 members of the 32 management teams.

2. Open-ended responses. In addition to responding to the scaled items, the leaders and members responded in writing to a series of open-ended questions which accompanied the items described above. These open-ended questions included:

- What are the current strengths of the team?
- If you could change one thing in order to help the team function more effectively, what would it be?
- If you could discuss one issue in an open way, involving the total team in the discussion, what would that issue be?
- What one norm or practice does the team accept that keeps the team from functioning better?
- What are the strengths of the team's leadership?
- What does the leader do that keeps the team from functioning more effectively?

Responses to these open-ended questions were analyzed by a sociological research organization, Omni Research and Training of Denver, Colorado. The dominant themes were identified and tabulated through a computer-assisted ethnography package. Dominant themes comprise the second type of information collected on the 32 management teams.

3. Analysis/feedback sessions. Responses to the scaled items and the open-ended questions were collected from leaders and members of each team separately. These responses were analyzed, synthesized, and displayed in a report prepared separately for each of the 32 teams. Each team then met approximately three weeks after the data collection to examine their report, interpret the data, develop a shared understanding of the implications of these data for the team, and develop a plan for improving the team's performance.

These analysis/feedback sessions typically lasted six to 12 hours. What was said and what occurred during these analysis/feedback sessions is the third kind of information we have concerning the 32 management teams.

Drawing on these three types of information makes it possible to describe some of the learnings we've discovered so far. We'll limit ourselves to those conclusions that have emerged most strongly or most repeatedly, that tend to be reinforced by more than just one type of information, and in which we have developed the most confidence.

PERCEIVED STRENGTHS OF TEAMS

Leaders and members are likely to agree on what the strengths of the team are. There is a very tightly interrelated set of factors likely to be viewed as present among the successful management teams we have studied. In fact, we have come to view these features as so fundamental to an effectively functioning team that you are simply not likely to encounter teams who rate themselves low on these factors or who describe themselves as having serious problems in these categories. The three interrelated factors are a clear, elevating goal; competent team members; and standards of excellence.

These factors are consistently rated high by the 32 management teams we have studied. They are most frequently mentioned in response to the question: What are the current strengths of this team? The nature of our sample almost precludes teams with serious problems in any of these three categories. Teams with severe deficiencies in any of these categories either (1) simply don't survive very long or (2) don't voluntarily place themselves into self-analysis and self-improvement programs, and consequently haven't shown up in our sample. To be sure, we have encountered teams that have some ambiguity about their goal. But this ambiguity is usually not severe and represents relatively minor differences in the way team members conceptualize the goal.

To create an effective team, we suggest you begin with the following three building blocks: *First*, make sure that the goal is clear, the performance objective crystallized. Formulate a clearly defined need—a goal to be achieved or a purpose to be served—that justifies the existence of the team. Make that goal something that challenges individual limits and abilities and that represents an opportunity for an exceptional level of achievement. Make the goal something noble or worthwhile, something from which people can derive a sense of identity.

Then select good people, members who possess the essential skills and abilities to accomplish the team's objectives. Make whatever investment is necessary to obtain talented people who are capable of collaborating effectively with each other.

Finally, foster high standards of excellence. Promote clear visualization, not only of the goal attainment, but of how that goal can be attained in a new way, a way that establishes a new performance standard for teams.

With these fundamentals established, you then can turn your attention to avoiding the common problems that beset teams—those reviewed in the following section.

THE MOST COMMON PROBLEMS

When team members examine the problems besetting the team, or the conditions that need to be changed for the team to perform more effectively, the problems most frequently identified involve the following areas:

1. Unified commitment. Especially intense among teams that are struggling, but more likely than anything else to be noted as a problem across all teams, is unified commitment. Team members are likely to be perceived as putting individual objectives above the team goal. The items in the unified commitment category are also the lowest rated by team members. The response that is far more frequent than any other response is that the team allows individuals to place self-interest above team-interest. Tolerating members who are more self-oriented than team-oriented is the most common complaint about what the team does.

Similarly, when asked what one issue team members would like to discuss in an open way—involving the total team in the discussion—that one issue is more frequently connected with unified commitment than with any other category. Although Chapter 5 discusses the ways team leaders tend to handle this problem, we have found that team members are frequently more sensitive to the problem than are team leaders and often would appreciate the opportunity to discuss this problem in an honest and candid manner with the team.

2. External support and recognition. The second common problem confronting teams is the tendency for both team leaders and members to feel that the team is not sufficiently recognized for its accomplishments and that reward and incentive structures are not tied to team performance. This problem is likely to be reported both by teams performing unusually well and by teams functioning ineffectively. The problem is intensified at both ends of the performance continuum but is commonly reported by teams in the mid-range of the performance continuum. The basic problem is the perception by team members and leaders that the team is given performance objectives to achieve but is not recognized or rewarded as a team. Instead, reward and recognition usually comes, if at all, for individual performance. The interaction between this problem and the problems associated with unified commitment is, we assume, obvious.

3. Collaboration. Team members, much more so than team leaders, are likely to complain about the absence of open, honest communication. The complaints tend to identify a climate in which secrecy occurs; there is limited dialogue among the team members; even essential information is not openly shared; there are cliques and hidden agendas; and caution and maneuvering prevail.

Our involvement in analysis/feedback sessions with management teams has led us to two conclusions with respect to this common problem. First, the extent to which a collaborative climate is present in a team is very much influenced by the team leader. In fact, members tend to mirror the collaborative style of the leader. Second, a positive collaborative climate is more likely to develop within teams that spend considerable time and energy in examining and seeking ways to improve their own working relationships.

PERCEIVED STRENGTHS OF TEAM LEADERS

Of the many positive characteristics of team leadership we reviewed in Chapter 9, there are two that might be regarded as standout features of effective team leaders. These characteristics don't necessarily occur together. Either of them can give a team leader a distinctive area of strength in the perception of team members.

First is the team leader who exhibits a *personal commitment* to the team's goal. This is the action-oriented leader who demonstrates his/ her commitment to the goal by investing the same, or greater, time and energy than is being asked of the members. This is not the leader who confronts the team with the problem and then walks away saying, "If you need any help, give me a call." This is the leader who demonstrates commitment by action rather than words.

Second is the leader who gives team members the necessary *autonomy* to achieve results. In Chapter 9 we emphasized a characteristic of effective team leadership as building a climate that permits failure. Similarly, the management teams we have studied show a special appreciation for leaders who provide autonomy to team members. These leaders recognize that failure occurs occasionally as a natural by-product of effort, especially that effort which is expended in pursuit of unusual aspirations. Leaders who develop their members by providing opportunities and who encourage members to stretch their abilities possess a positive characteristic that sets them apart from other team leaders.

TWO BLIND SPOTS OF TEAM LEADERS

There are two interesting highlights in the data we have accumulated about team leadership. They involve two of the most frequent complaints voiced about team leaders by members. They also involve the two lowest rated items out of all the leadership items in our measures. And, interestingly, they represent two of the items on which the greatest disagreement exists between the ratings of the team leader and the average ratings of team members. They surface repeatedly in the analysis/feedback sessions.

First, the most severe complaint about team leadership from team members involves leaders who are unwilling to confront and resolve issues associated with inadequate performance by team members. Leaders see themselves as far more active in this area than do team members. Of course, team members are more likely to be sensitive to inadequate performance problems, since they are more directly and continually impacted by the problems. Their sense of frustration with individual performance problems is greater, and their desire to confront and resolve the issue is more intense.

A close second in intensity, and by far the most frequent response to the question, "What does the leader do that keeps the team from functioning more effectively?" is that the leader dilutes the team's efforts with too many priorities. Leaders who take on too many objectives and priorities for the team, who unquestioningly accept whatever tasks are given them, whose career aspirations are such that they will overload the team and dilute its effort rather than protect the team's standards and potential for significant achievement are the targets of this complaint. Especially objectionable are leaders who put constant pressure on the team to perform on a never-ending line of objectives, each of which is described by the leader as "critical," but who applies this pressure out of a concern for his/her own present and future well-being rather than out of a concern for the quality and significance of the performance objective itself.

DIFFERENCES IN LEADER-MEMBER PERCEPTIONS

What are the aspects of teams and teamwork that leaders and members are most likely to see differently? When we explored the data for the answer to this question, we found several small surprises and one very large one. When we examined the scaled items, and compared the mean member rating across all teams with the mean leader rating across all teams, the following items produced the greatest discrepancy between the member ratings and the leader ratings:

- Team members are capable of collaborating effectively with each other.
- Achieving our team goal is a higher priority than any individual objective.
- Team members are willing to devote whatever effort is necessary to achieve team success.
- Our communication system has opportunities for team members to raise issues not on the formal agenda.
- Our communication system has information which is easily accessible.
- Our decision-making process encourages judgments based on factual and objective data.

These half dozen items point to some interesting differences in the perceptions of leaders and members. *First,* there are differences in the perception of how capable of collaboration team members are. Note that this item is in the category "competent team members" rather than the category "collaborative climate." *Second,* two of the items deal with "unified commitment." There are differences in the perceptions of leaders and members in terms of how committed team members are to achieving the goal. *Third,* the final three items deal with "results-driven structure" and, more specifically, the nature of the communication that is occurring within the team.

The major surprise in the data is this: In all six items, the team leader rates the team much higher than do team members. In other words, team leaders are much more likely to describe these characteristics as true of the team than are team members. Our conversations with leaders and members reinforce an emerging conclusion from these data. Team leaders have a tendency to overestimate how smoothly the team is functioning. Team leaders are often surprised at the nature or severity of problems that surface during the analysis/ feedback sessions.

The patterns in our data contain an important message for team leaders. It is relatively easy for leaders to become somewhat removed from the intimate workings of the team, whether because their attention becomes fixed on other matters or simply because the leader is less likely to experience the problems directly. Recall how the team leaders in our original interviews told us how important it was for the leader to create a climate in which negative information was shared, for the leader to be a good listener, for the leader to stay in close touch with the team. And when those leaders talked about how constant and intensive this effort must be, they were expressing a principle they clearly understood from very valuable experience.

TEAMWORK AS VIEWED FROM THE INSIDE

If you take a look at what team members say about each other, another interesting insight emerges. The standards for effective teamwork within the team are often more rigorous than those imposed from above or outside. For example, the most consistent complaints team members have about each other are: team members who make personal objectives a higher priority than the team goals; team members who do not take an active enough role in providing leadership for the team; and team members who do not respond constructively to feedback from others. And with regard to the open-ended question "What might this individual do to contribute more effectively to the team's success?" the responses fall into similar categories: comments that suggest ways in which the individual can collaborate more effectively with other team members; comments that urge or demand that the individual commit more time or energy to the collective effort; and comments that suggest that the individual concentrate more on the results to be attained than on political or territorial issues.

On the flip side, when team members are rating or describing the individual contributions that other members make to team success, they focus disproportionately on competence and high standards of excellence. In fact, 44% of all positive comments about individuals who contributed to the success of the team had to do with unusual levels of competence and high standards of excellence. When competence and standards are directed toward achieving the team goal, these are appreciated more by team members than are any other individual factors.

The lesson we have learned repeatedly, from examining the data and from observing teams analyzing themselves, is the one that Elliot Richardson reminded us of early in the research: The one concept that everyone can understand and appreciate is excellence. If the goal is clear, worthwhile, and challenging, team members will probably do a better job of energizing and commanding themselves and fellow team members than will sources above or outside the team.

We continue to discover new things about teams and teamwork every time we sit down with a team and every time we examine our small but growing data base. Almost everything we discover makes us more optimistic. We are more optimistic about what can be achieved through collaborative effort. We are more optimistic about the clarity and consistency of the conclusions that will emerge from studying collaboration. And we are more optimistic about the basic instincts of people engaged in collaboration with each other.

Underlying this optimism is a pattern that has become increasingly crystallized: The fundamental factor, the point of departure, the thing that shapes everything that follows is the goal. All that people have to invest in a collective effort, in terms of usable resources, is time and energy. These are the resources we all have available to commit. But they are, for each of us, limited. If we are asked to commit these resources on trivial matters, or for the sake of achieving someone else's personal ambitions, we feel that we are being "used." And we are. But if we commit these resources to something significant, something that will last, something that renders the expenditure of time and energy worthwhile, then the stage is set for effective teamwork. Optimism will prevail because, quite literally, anything is possible. What is most likely is another confirmation of Ralph Waldo Emerson's statement that "every great and commanding moment in the annals of the world is the triumph of some enthusiasm." Such is the spirit of teamwork.

NOTE

1. The categories, number of items per category, and Cronbach's alphas associated with the items by category, are listed below:

Clear, elevating goal, 6 items, .85
Results-driven structure, 8 items, .80
Competent team members, 4 items, .81
Unified commitment, 3 items, .86
Collaborative climate, 4 items, .84
Standards of excellence, 3 items, .72
External support and recognition, 7 items, .79
Principled leadership, 13 items, .88

REFERENCES

Adler, P., & Adler, P. (in press). Intense loyalty in organizations: A case study of college athletics. *Administrative Science Quarterly.*

Andre de la Porte, P. C. (1974, September–October). Group norms: Key to building a winning team. *Personnel, 51* (5), 60–67.

Anundsen, K. (1979, February). Building teamwork and avoiding backlash: Keys to developing managerial women. *Managerial Review, 68,* 55–58.

Arendt, H. (1958). *The human condition.* Chicago: University of Chicago Press.

Belbin, R. M. (1981). *Management teams: Why they succeed or fail.* New York: John Wiley.

Bennis, W., & Nanus, B. (1985). *Leaders: The strategies for taking charge.* New York: Harper and Row.

Burns, J. M. (1978). *Leadership.* New York: Harper and Row.

Chlewinski, Z. (1981). Group and individual decisions in task situations: Aspirations and achievement. *Polish Psychological Bulletin, 12* (2), 115–124.

Cohen, S. (1982, April). A monkey on the back, a lump in the throat. *Inside Sports, 4* (4), 20.

Coleman, R. (1987). *An examination and synthesis of factors central to team success.* Unpublished manuscript, University of Denver, Denver, CO.

Crosby, P. B. (1979). *Quality is free.* New York: McGraw-Hill.

Dewey, J. (1910). *How we think.* Boston: D. C. Heath.

Dyer, W. G. (1977). *Team building: Issues and alternatives.* Reading, MA: Addison-Wesley.

Eichhorn, S. F. (1974). *Becoming: The actualization of individual differences in five student health teams.* New York: Institute for Health Team Development, Montefiore Hospital and Medical Center, Bronx, NY.

Fiedler, F. E., & Chemers, M. M. (1974). *Leadership and effective management.* Glenview, IL: Scott, Foresman.

Galagan, P. (1986, November). Work teams that work. *Training and Development Journal, 40,* 35.

Garfield, C. A. (1986). *Peak performers.* New York: Avon Books.

Garfield, C. A., & Bennett, H. Z. (1984). *Peak performance: Mental training techniques of the world's greatest athletes.* New York: Warner Books.

Gavin, J. F., & McPhail, S. M. (1978, April-May-June). Intervention and evaluation: A proactive team approach to OD. *Journal of Applied Behavioral Science, 14,* 175–194.

Glaser, B., & Strauss, A. (1967). *The discovery of grounded theory: Strategies for qualitative research.* New York: Aldine.

Grading merit pay. (1988, November 14). *Newsweek,* pp. 45–46.

Gudykunst, W. B., & Ting-Toomey, S. (1988). *Culture and interpersonal communication.* Newbury Park, CA: Sage.

Hart, C. W. L. (1988). The power of unconditional service guarantees. *Harvard Business Review, 66* (4), 54–62.

Hastings, C., Bixby, P., & Chaudry-Lawton, R. (1987). *The superteam solution: Successful teamworking in organizations.* San Diego: University Associates.

Hirokawa, R., & Poole, M. S. (1986). *Communication and group decision-making.* Beverly Hills, CA: Sage.

Hollingsworth, A. T., Meglino, B. M., & Shaner, M. C. (1979, August). Coping with team trauma. *Management Review, 68,* 48–50.

Holusha, J. (1987, December 29). A new spirit at U.S. auto plants. *New York Times,* pp. 25–26.

Jennings, E. E. (1960). *An anatomy of leadership.* New York: Harper & Brothers.

Keidel, R. (1985). *Game plans.* New York: Berkley Books.

Keidel, R. (1988, November 27). Going beyond "I'm O.K., you're O.K." *New York Times,* p. 2.

Kiechel, W., III. (1988, November 21). The case against leaders. *Fortune, 118* (122), 217–220.

Kiefer, C. F., & Senge, P. M. (1984). Metanoic organizations. In J. D. Adams (Ed.), *Transforming Work* (pp. 109–122). Alexandria, VA: Miles River Press. Based on C. F. Kiefer & P. M. Senge (1982). Metanoic organizations in the transition to a sustainable society. *Technological Forecasting and Social Change, 2* (22).

Kohn, A. (1986). *No contest: The case against competition.* Boston: Houghton-Mifflin.

Kotter, J. P. (1988). *The leadership factor.* New York: Free Press.

Likert, R. (1976, March). Improving cost performance with cross-functional teams. *Management Review, 65,* 36–42.

Perrow, C. (1984). *Normal accidents: Living with high-risk technologies.* New York: Basic Books.

Quickel, S. W. (1988, June). A delicate operation. *Business Month,* pp. 40–44.

Reich, R. R. (1987). *Tales of a new America.* New York: Time Books.

Sherwin, D. S. (1976, May-June). Management of objectives. *Harvard Business Review, 54,* 149–160.

Sonnenfeld, J. (1988). *The hero's farewell: What happens when CEOs retire.* New York: Oxford University Press.

Straus, D. B. (1986, April). Collaborating to understand without being a "wimp." *Negotiation Journal, 2,* 156.

Sugarman, B. (1968). Social norms in teenage boys' peer groups: A study of their implications for achievement and conduct in four London schools. *Human Relations, 21* (1), 41–58.

Sullivan, J. B. (1988). *Team origins.* Denver: Performance Training Corp.

Tichy, N. M., & Devanna, M. A. (1986). *The transformational leader.* New York: John Wiley.

Toffler, A. (1980). *The third wave.* New York: Bantam.

Truell, G. F. (1984). *Building and managing productive work teams.* Buffalo, NY: PAT Publications.

Waterman, R. H., Jr. (1987). *The renewal factor.* New York: Bantam.

Waterman, R. H., Jr., & Peters, T. (1982). *In search of excellence*. New York: Harper and Row.

Wirth maps out war on "greenhouse effect." (1988. July 29). *Denver Post*, p. 1.

Witkin, R. (1987. September 19). F.A.A. says Delta had poor policies on crew training. *New York Times*, p. 1.

Zaleznick, A. (1977). Managers and leaders: Are they different? *Harvard Business Review*, *53* (3), 73.

Zimbardo, P., & Ebbeson, E. (1969). *Influencing attitudes and changing behavior*. Reading. MA: Addison-Wesley.

INDEX

ABOUT THE AUTHORS

Carl E. Larson, Ph.D., is Professor of Speech Communication and past Dean of Social Sciences at the University of Denver. Coauthor of five books on communication theory and research, Dr. Larson specializes in applying communication principles in concrete problem situations. He has conducted and/or consulted on social science research projects with agencies of state and national governments and with corporations.

Frank M. J. LaFasto, Ph.D., is Vice President for Human Resource Planning and Development for Baxter Healthcare Corporation, a position that involves him in succession planning, performance measurement, executive development, and selection standards. An author and guest lecturer on management issues, Dr. LaFasto has extensive experience in building effective management teams.

NOTES

NOTES